ANNE HUTCHINSON

Unsung Heroine of History

(1591 - 1643)

BOOKS
THAT HEAL
AND INSPIRE

ANNE HUTCHINSON

Unsung Heroine of History

by

Bianca A. Leonardo
and
Winnifred K. Rugg

Tree of Life Publications
Joshua Tree CA 92252

Ph. 760-366-3695; Fax: 366-3596
TREE OF LIFE PUBLICATIONS
P.O. Box 126
Joshua Tree, CA 92252-0126

New edition, ISBN: 0-930852-30-3.

Copyright © 1995 by Bianca Leonardo
Publication date: December 1995

Tree of Life Publications
Post Office Box 126
Joshua Tree, CA 92252

Manufactured in the United States of America

Library of Congress Cataloging-in-Publication Data

Leonardo, Bianca.
    Anne Hutchinson : unsung heroine of history / by Bianca A.
Leonardo and Winnifred K. Rugg. — New ed.
        p.   cm.
    Rev. ed. of : Unafraid / by Winnifred K. Rugg, 1930.
    Includes bibliographical references (p.   ) and index.
    ISBN 0-930852-30-3 (paperback) : $19.95
    1. Hutchinson, Anne Marbury, 1591-1643.   2. Puritans—
Massachusetts—Biography.   I. Rugg, Winnifred King.   II. Rugg,
Winnifred King. Unafraid.   III. Title.
F67.H92L46   1995
973.22'092—dc20
[B]   95-3439

Dedicated

To All Women Everywhere

Who Yearn To Be Free To Reach

Their Highest Potential

Acknowledgments

MY THANKS, first of all, to Anne Hutchinson, who inspired me from the time I first read about her incredible life and death; to Winnifred King Rugg, for the original book — who, in 1930, suffered a lack of recognition; to Rev. Midge Anthony, for the new title and other help; to Shauna Russ and Al Gilbert, my careful typesetters; to Betty Hann, my devoted assistant; and to Lynn Souder, of the C.I.P. division of the Copyright Office, for her cooperation.

Bianca Leonardo

CONTENTS

About Bianca Leonardo

After finding an old copy of the first edition of this work by Winnifred King Rugg (1930 publication date — different title), Ms. Leonardo set out to edit, modernize, and amplify it. The epilogue ("The Spirit of Anne Speaks") is her work.

Ms. Leonardo is also an editor and publisher with a background of twenty-five years in this field. Earlier careers were journalism, radio news reporting, professor of English, mother, and homemaker. She served in the U.S. Army as a writer for Stars and Stripes, and Yank magazine.

No picture of Anne Hutchinson exists (only a statue, a photo of which is included here). Neither picture nor biography of Winnifred King Rugg could be found.

ANNE HUTCHINSON
"Morality on Fire with Emotion"

Statue by Cyrus E. Dallin

State House
Boston, Massachusetts
From this spot (General Court of Massachusetts),
she was exiled in 1638.

PREFACE

AFTER AN OLD FASHION

In writings of earlier days, the days of Anne Hutchinson for example, the cream of a book was its preamble. Here writers were in the habit of giving a detailed advertisement of their wares, fearing, perhaps, that their readers might not endure to the end of the book. Thus, in case a similar misfortune should befall this book, we assume the privilege of an old fashion in providing Anne Hutchinson with a formal introduction.

"Why write about Anne Hutcinson?" some ask. Some have even gone so far as to enquire, "Who was she?" *She lived almost 400 years ago, in the Massachusetts Bay Colony. If she had been of the male gender, all American history books would have included this dynamic personality.*

Telling who Anne Hutchinson was is objective enough. To define an individuality, to sublimate the essence of a personality, is the prime reason for putting a man or a woman on paper, whether it be in actual biography, or in the imaginary biography that is fiction. To say that Anne Hutchinson was the most conspicuous woman of her time in America gives a reason for writing about her. Because she was so constituted of untiring energy, unsleeping will, high intelligence, fervor, a silver tongue, a great capacity for friendship and splendid egotism, she could not have helped being conspicuous anywhere, anytime.

Anne Hutchinson has been called by many names. From "the New England Jezebel" to "a type of Joan of Arc" run the epithets wholeheartedly applied by enemies or friends. In between lie such labels as "that proud dame," "that Athaliah[1]," "a notorious Imposter," "a dayngerous Instrument of the Devell raysed up by Sathan," "a Breeder of Heresies," "a persuasive advocate of the right of individual judgement," "a she-Gamaliel[2]," "a New England Vittoria Colonna[3]," and "a dear saint and servant of God." (That last is her husband speaking. Poor man, he suffered more on her account than anyone else!)

A character who they can interpret so diversely provokes examination. Anne Hutchinson partook in some ways of the spirit of her time and of her fellow-pioneers in New England. Still, in other important ways, she stands out against the background of primitive Massachusetts. Anne was at swords' points with its leaders, sinewed with the courage to tell how she differed, and endowed with the personality to make what she said effective. Clearly Anne was an individual; there was something "in" her.

Incidentally, what she did was interesting. Her life was a melodrama. Anne left her comfortable home in England for conscience' sake and persuaded her family to come to America. She became the leader of a powerful party in the colony and she collided with the clergy. They tried her before the General Court of Massachusetts, they expelled her from the colony and excommunicated her from the church. Anne helped to found a freer settlement in a new wilderness and in later years she sought still another refuge. Finally Anne perished, with almost all her family, massacred by Indians. This is a tale of adventure, strife and tragedy rarely told of any English gentlewoman.

What Anne Hutchinson stood for is another reason for examining her history. She was one of the few feminists of her day. She founded what was, in essence, the first women's club in America. Though the meetings held in her house were primarily for religious instruction, they were the forerunners of today's gatherings. The spirit of Anne Hutchinson has existed in the hundreds of thousands of meetings where women convene to improve themselves or the rest of the world. The Hutchinson house, which stood at what is now the northerly corner of Washington and School Streets, Boston, was the birthplace of the women's clubs of America.

Her history has made Anne Hutchinson to stand for

the principle of free speech — a principle always glorious in prospect or retrospect, and always bothersome, even terrifying, when in action. How much of her freedom of speech came from an active, conscious conviction of the right of dissenting minorities to voice their opinion, and how much from a subconscious desire for self-expression, is a question to be discussed later. The fact remains that she was a participant in the five-hundred-year-old drama of freedom vs. authority. She did dissent from the opinion of the majority of the clergy in New England. Because she insisted upon expressing her dissent, they made her suffer for it. Martyrdom is always a good ticket to immortality. Today, many who are not in sympathy with Anne Hutchinson's specific tenets will say, "I do not agree with a word that you say, but I will defend to the death, your right to say it."

Anne, the individual, is our theme, outlined against the background of Puritan New England. We shall see her giving help to the sick and needy and impetuously striving to impress her ideas on the Boston congregation. She is occupied with counseling, expounding, and riding on the high wave of popularity. She ably defends her views before the most experienced debaters of the colony. Then, inquisition style, they badger and exile her. Driven from Boston, she carries the banner of her dauntless independence to Rhode Island and, finally, to primitive New York. There, she and most of her children are massacred by Indians.

A generous, tremendously active, and energetic woman, she is ardent, imperious, independent, sharp-witted and sharp-tongued, persistent, magnetic, egotistic — and unafraid.

She differed from the leaders of the colony in that she had no fear. They, being afraid, persecuted her. Fear, mated to power, produces intolerance.

In the back of the book is a list of the authorities we have consulted in this study of Anne Hutchinson. John Winthrop and Reverend Thomas Weld first told her story in their own extenuation. It was a short history with a long name beginning, *A Short History of the Rise, Reign and Ruin of the Antinomians, Familists and Libertines that infected the churches in New England, etc.* Anne Hutchinson's great-great-grandson, Lieutenant-Governor Thomas Hutchinson, told it in his *History of Massachusetts*; George E. Ellis wrote a *Life of Anne Hutchinson*, published in 1845 in Jared Sparks's *Library of American Biography*. Since then, her life has not been written by itself. However, she has formed an important section in such books as Ellis's *Puritan Age and Rule*, and *Three*

Episodes in American History, by Charles Francis Adams. Also, her name can be found in most of the detailed histories of New England. All these are largely concerned with the four years that she spent in Boston, from 1634 to 1638. Yet, she lived fifty-two years. What of the other forty-eight years?

In front of the State House in Boston, stands a majestic statue of Anne Hutchinson wrought by Cyrus E. Dallin*. She holds her head high, her lips proudly curved, poised erect and imperious. One hand is holding her Bible and the other rests on the shoulder of a young daughter. When the church rejected her, she had proclaimed, "Better to be cast out of the church than to deny Christ." Her stance, now frozen in time, recalls that very day when she last stood on the threshold of that church. She is uplifted, touched with prophetic fire. She is unafraid. The location of her statue illustrates an interesting example of the irony of history. It now occupies a place of honor in front of the present meeting place of the General Court of Massachusetts that cast her out of their jurisdiction so many years before.

A tablet is found in the First Church of Boston that honors Anne Hutchinson. In Wollaston, Massachusetts,

---

* See frontispiece in this volume.

is another marking the spot whence she started on the exile's pilgrimage to Rhode Island.

These memorials of Anne Hutchinson, provocative as they are to one who stops to notice them, do not even suggest all there is to know about her. Anne the woman may be discovered, as well as Anne the pioneer, Anne the troublemaker, or Anne the martyr. Certain episodes of the nine years she lived in America are documented. However, no useful diarist or note taker has handed down a report of the forty-three years that Anne spent in England. We can wrest a poor pittance of recorded facts about her and her family from parish registers, college rolls, and court records. Also, she herself later gave accounts of the spiritual experiences that she passed through before leaving England. We know other facts about life overall in those last days of Queen Elizabeth's reign and the days of the earlier Stuarts. By combining these two sources of information, we may glimpse a real woman against an historic background. In this search, recorded history has been the guide, imagination only a lantern.

With this letter of introduction, we, after the old fashion, beg to commend the reader to the society of one who, as Dr. Richard Garnett has said of Emerson, possessed the individual Puritan characteristic, "morality on fire with emotion."

1. Athaliah: a Biblical character, mentioned in II Kings 11:1-3, 13-16, and 20. She was the daughter of Ahab and Jezebel and mother of Ahaziah, ruler of Judah. Ahaziah, like his grandfather Ahab, was a worshiper of Baal. When they slew Ahaziah at the command of Jehu, and Athaliah heard of it, "she arose and destroyed all the seed royal." (KJV). They killed Athaliah at the command of the priest Jehaiadu.

2. Gamaliel: A Pharisee and celebrated doctor of the law, who gave prudent worldly advice in the Sanhedrin respecting the treatment of the followers of Jesus (Acts 5:34). He was the preceptor of Paul, before he was so renamed. Acts 22:3 ". . . brought up in this city (Celicia) at the feet of Gamaliel, . . ." Hence, a "she-Gamaliel" would mean that Anne was an outstanding religious teacher.

3. Vittoria Colonna was an Italian poet. Born in 1490, in Naples of an aristocratic family, she married the Marquis Ferrera, who was killed in battle. After his death, she wrote some 100 poems to his memory. They are religious-oriented. She had a long and platonic relationship with Michelangelo. She spent the latter part of her life in a convent.

PROLOGUE

Saint Paul's Consistory, London, November 5, in the year of our Lord 1578, and of the reign of Queen Elizabeth the twentieth.

The Ecclesiastical Court presided over by Bishop Aylmer of London holds conference with Francis Marbury, deacon, late of Northampton, previously imprisoned for his preaching, released, and again arrested. With Bishop Alymer sit Sir Owen Hopton, Archdeacon Mullins, and other members of the High Commission.

They fill the council room. Occupying the seats in the center are eminent representatives of the clergy with laymen of good rank. Distinguished among the former is my Lord Edmund Scambler, Bishop of Peterborough, who not long before had ordained young Marbury and had time to regret it. In the rear of the room and along the walls are less important members of the laity, many of whom show sympathy for the accused.

Before the bar stands Marbury himself, an ardent, headlong young man of twenty-two. Under the cross-examination his face lights up with the joy of battle. His chin is out-thrust, his head high, his eye level and fearless.

Wit and tongue are both ready to his command, so he can afford to smile at the heavy artillery of his examiners. Ponderously come the questions; quick and keen are the answers. Sometimes they call forth a burst of laughter from the crowd, and the High Commissioners grow apoplectic.

Bishop Aylmer proceeds to the examination.

BISHOP — Marbury, where were you since your last release?

MARBURY — At Northampton.

BISHOP — That was the place whither you were specially forbidden to go, for there you did all the harm.

MARBURY — I neither rightly may be inhibited the place, neither have I done harm there, but I trust good.

BISHOP — As you say, sir.

MARBURY — Not so, but I refer me to the judgment of God's church there.

BISHOP — The last time you found more favor than you deserved and more than, possibly, you shall find thereafter, and yet you have vaunted that you have rattled up the Bishop of Peterborough, and so you would me. Well, sir, now you are come, what have you to say to my Lord Peterborough or to me?

MARBURY — Nothing but God save you both.

BISHOP — Nothing? Why, you were wont to bark

much of dumb dogs. Are you weary of your part?

MARBURY — I come not to accuse but to defend. But, because you urge me for advantage, *I say the Bishops of London are guilty of the death of as many souls as have perished by the ignorance of the ministers of their making whom they know to be unable.*

BISHOP — Whom such have I made?

MARBURY — I accuse not you particularly because I know not your estate. If you have, you shall bear this condemnation.

BISHOP — The proposition is false. If it were in Cambridge, it would be hissed out of the schools.

MARBURY — Then you had need to hire hissers!

RECORDER — Marbury, use my Lord more reverently. He is a peer of the Realms; I perceive your words are puffed up with pride.

MARBURY — Sir, I speak but the truth to him. I reverence him so far as he is reverend, and I pray God to teach him to die.

BISHOP — Thou speakest of making ministers. The Bishop of Peterborough was never more deceived in his life, than when he admitted thee to be a Preacher in Northampton.

MARBURY — Like enough in some sense. I pray God the scales may fall from his eyes.

BISHOP — Thou takest upon thyself to be a preacher, but there is nothing in thee; thou art a very ass, an idiot and a fool. Thou art courageous, nay, thou art impudent! By my troth, I think he be mad, he careth for nobody.

MARBURY — Sir, I take exception against swearing judges. I praise God I am not mad, but sorry to see you so out of temper.

BISHOP (breathless) — Did you ever hear one so impudent? (The Bishop gets his breath, then continues.) This fellow would have a preacher in every church.

MARBURY — So would Saint Paul.

BISHOP — Where wouldst thou have them?

MARBURY — In Cambridge, in Oxford, in the Inns of Court, yea, and some in prisons, if there wanted more. We doing our part, the Lord would do His part.

BISHOP — The prison might suffice for living for thee, but where is the living for them?

MARBURY — A man might cut a good large thong out of your hide and the rest, and it would not be missed.

BISHOP — Thou shalt dispose our livings orderly.

ARCHDEACON MULLINS — Sir, in the beginning of Her Majesty's reign, there was a defect of able men, and the Church was constrained to take such as it could get upon commendation of noblemen.

MARBURY — I speak of a later date. As for noblemen,

they are no sureties for us. And for the defect you speak of, it cannot dispense with the absolute words: *He must be able to teach.* There is no such clause as, *'Except there be a defect.'*

ARCHDEACON MULLINS — Why then, you will have a preacher or nobody. So, the Church will be unserved.

MARBURY — *It is better to have nothing than that which God would not have.*

BISHOP — How proveth thou that God would not have them when we can get no better?

MARBURY — Did He not say, 'Because thou refuseth knowledge, I will also refuse thee, that thou shalt be no priest to me?'

BISHOP — Thou art an overthwart, proud, Puritan knave, and thou wilt have thine own saying to die, but thou shalt repent it.

MARBURY — I am no Puritan. I beseech you be good to me. I have been twice in prison, but I know not why.

BISHOP — Where was he before?

KEEPER OF THE GAOL-HOUSE — With me, my Lord.

BISHOP — Have him to the Marshalsea.[1] There he shall cope with the Papists.

MARBURY — I am to go whither it pleaseth God, but remember God's judgments. You do me open wrong. I pray God to forgive you.[2]

Nearly sixty years later Francis Marbury's daughter, banished from Massachusetts and excommunicated from the church in Boston, proclaimed the spirit of her father in the face of her enemies, saying, as she passed from their presence: "The Lord judgeth not as man judgeth."

The daughter of the "proud, Puritan knave" was Anne Hutchinson. She inherited his free spirit.

1. A prison in Southwark where Catholics were confined in the reign of Elizabeth.

2. This prologue is a condensed version of the report of Marbury's examination before the High Commission, as written down by Marbury himself in a rare volume made up of forty-two tracts by *"divers godly and learned in our time which stand for and desire the reformation of our church in Discipline and Ceremonies."* There is no printer's name, place, or date on the volume, but Dexter assigns 1590 as the probable date of publication. Marbury's tract, in which he says his trial took place on *"the 5 of November last past, Anno 1578,"* must have been written as early as 1579. It is signed Francis Marburie. He writes himself Merburie and Marburie in the text.

The whole matter has been clearly set forth by Frederick L. Gay in a paper included in the Massachusetts Historical Society *Collections*, volume 48, page 281. Mr. Gay's evidence is based on the *Biographical Register of Christ's College, Cambridge, 1505-1905,* by John Peile; on a letter written by Francis Marbury to Lord Burleigh, preserved in the Cecil Papers, CLXVII, 109, on the *Records of Ordination* in the Bishop of London's Registry, Liber *Ordinationum, 1578-1628,* and on the Parish Register of Alford, County Lincoln.

I

ALFORD, ENGLAND, 1605

In the twenty-seven years after his trial before the High Commission, Francis Marbury made peace with his Bishop. He preached at Alford in Lincolnshire six or seven years, got into trouble again, and the Bishop again silenced him. In vain he pleaded for reinstatement. He married twice, had fourteen children christened and four of them buried, all the time living in Alford. Then, after fifteen years of enforced silence, Bishop Vaughan appointed Marbury to a church in London.

Francis Marbury's second wife, whom he married two or three years before his Alford preaching met with disfavor, was the mother of Anne. She was Bridget, daughter of John Dryden, Esq., of Canons Ashby in Northamptonshire, near the town where Francis Marbury first ran afoul of the Bishops. The Drydens were a strong Puritan family, though one of them, the poet Dryden, Bridget's grandnephew, showed in later years great facility at turning his coat.[1] Francis Marbury was a young widower with one little girl, Susan, when he married into the Dryden family.

By the time Marbury received the good news that the

Bishop had appointed him to a London living, his family consisted of ten children. They were Susan, John, Anne, who was fourteen that summer, Francis, Emme, Erasmus, Bridget, Jeremoth, Daniel, and Elizabeth. Susan was twenty; Elizabeth was an infant of nine months. As for the rest—well, does it matter? Our interest lies in Anne, whom they christened July 20, 1591. If her parents followed the custom of the time in having their child baptized three days after birth, she was born July 17.

Of the Dryden contingent Anne was the eldest girl; her brother John was a year and a half her senior. Two other children had been in the second brood, but Marbury had laid them beside his first wife, Elizabeth Moore, and her two babes.

It must have been no small task to transplant this family. They were leaving behind the deliberate life of a Lincolnshire market town. The London of Court and Parliament, of merchant princes and adventurers, of playhouses and shops, great churches and unspeakable kennels was their future.

"What will London be like?" the younger children might ask sister Anne. Anne's eyes would flash. "What is London like?" she would cry. "It is a great, great city where you can see King James riding out in a glittering coach with the Queen. Lords and ladies and soldiers in armor parade with them. The streets are full of people.

Cheapside is like a street of gold, lined with the shops of goldsmiths. You can see a great bridge over the river Thames with houses on it and shops where you can buy anything, whatever you want. You can see ships that have come from foreign lands. You can see earls' houses and Father's own church!"

"What will Father's church be like?" a child would ask, pressing closer to her sister.

"'Tis an old church called Saint Martin's Vintry, and we shall live in the rectory close by and see Father wearing a surplice and preaching in the pulpit every Sunday. Every hour of every day, you will find something new to hear and see and to do."

For such a spirited, high-strung girl as Anne, the thought of going to London brought a fever of anticipation and, as in an actual fever, a heightened activity of mind. She was like a person transported, not distraught, but the more eager to throw herself wholeheartedly into the business of going. Her fourteen years at Alford she would dismiss as nothing. They had been years of learning lessons, of helping her mother and looking after little brothers and sisters. In her memory, a new baby was always in the cradle and younger Marburys tagging at her heels. She herself had tagged after the one half-sister who had lived and her own elder brother. She could not remember when she had not had to tie smaller children into their Holland coats each morning and hear their prayers each night.

Yet she had been happy enough in Alford. She had liked going with the children to the sand hills, whence they could see the gray line of the North Sea six miles away. After their hikes, they never tired of coming home to hear their father's glorious and appalling tale of the Spanish Armada fleeing northward under a southerly wind and the dread of Drake's men.

"The Lord sent His wind and scattered them," Francis Marbury always ended, solemnly quoting the commemoration medal. The wreck of the Spanish Armada happened three years before Anne was born, but Spanish salvage was seen in half the houses of Alford.

She had loved to climb to the top of the church tower. She looked over the flat country, raw green or dun, with its dykes and its windmills. Her father said it was like those of the Hollanders across the sea.

Of late there had been little chance for roaming the fields. John, young Frank and little Erasmus—poor youngster, afflicted with the Christian name so dear to his mother's kin, in token of grandfather Dryden's friendship with the famous Dutch scholar Erasmus—went to the grammar school. The very school that John Smith, who was to be a great explorer, had attended a decade before. She and her sisters stayed at home and learned from their father the small reading, writing, and figuring that were thought needful for gentlewomen in her part of the country. The example of Queen Elizabeth and some of her court ladies who studied Latin and Greek meant nothing to the small gentry of Lincolnshire. From her mother Anne learned to sew, to care for the sick, to prepare simples* and preserves, and to make home brew. She had lessons in deportment and in dancing. Common folk, even the children of the Hutchinsons, who were only shopkeepers, though richer than the Marburys, could dance boisterously on the village green. Nevertheless, Francis Marbury and Bridget Dryden might hire a traveling master to teach their children the pavon and the galliard, the tenternelle and coranto.

Probably there had been rare visits when Anne had gone to see her relatives. Fifteen miles to the northwest was the home of her father's older brother who had been knighted, Sir Edward Marbury of Girsby in the parish of Burgh-upon-Bain. Her mother's brother, Sir Erasmus Dryden, kept greater state at Canons Ashby, to the south in the neighboring shire of Northampton. Canons Ashby, with its terraces and giant cedars, its gardens and park, was one of the loveliest places in all England. When the

---

* Simple: A medicinal plant; a vegetable drug having only one ingredient.

heiress of Sir John Cope had married the schoolmaster, John Dryden, the property came into the Dryden family. These two became the grandparents of Anne Marbury.

Anne may have ridden pillion* behind her father down to the merchant city of Boston, twenty-four miles away. If so, her father showed her ships that traded with Norway and brought wealth to the town, so that they called it the Bristol of the east coast. He took her through crooked streets and bewildering lanes lined with peaked, projecting houses. He led her into Saint Botolph's Church and told her it was the most magnificent parish church in England. He affectionately called its curious tower, "Boston Stump." It was three hundred feet high, as tall as the highest tower of Lincoln Cathedral, and a mark both by land and by sea for all quarters thereabout. He pointed out the ancient and curious stones set at the four corners of the tower and cunningly carved with figures and scenes. Within the church were glorious windows of stained glass. A fair white marble font with a delicately carved cover surmounted by a dove was the loveliest thing Anne had ever seen. Lucky enough to be in Boston on some saint's day, she would see the procession in the streets when the guilds came out, and the mace, adorned with a cross, was

---

* Pillion: A pad or cushion placed behind a man's saddle, chiefly for a woman to ride on.

carried before the mayor to the church.

At the time, these sights had filled her childish mind with excitement, but now she deemed them commonplace for one about to go to London. She felt no regret at exchanging the level fields and marshes of her native Lincolnshire with its sleepy ways, even Boston with its ships and its church, for the crowded, eager world of action and ideas that she believed to be London. Sister Sue might weep over leaving old friends. Her mother might sigh at every diamond paned window and before every chimney piece. For her own part, the change could not come too soon. She wanted to run to meet it.

Good William Hutchinson would doubtless come and mourn on her doorstep, but though he was an honest youth, she could always beat him in an argument. Her blood did not quicken at the thought of him. She hoped that in London she would find someone who could say more than "Yea" and "Nay" and "I know not" to her sallies. She longed to sharpen her wit on someone else outside her own family. There was always her father, of course. No one could be a keener disputant than he. Still, though she believed that he secretly admired her swift tongue, she never quite dared to let herself go with him. But in London! Ah, in London, what might Anne see and hear and share! She might even share the sights — though not the talk — with William Hutchinson, if his father ever trusted him to go to London to buy goods for the shop.

She was glad that they were going to London on her father's account, too. She grew up with the knowledge that he was a disappointed man, cut short in his career as a preacher. His life, so far as she knew it, had been filled with baffled efforts at reinstatement.

The story was familiar enough to all the Marburys. The Bishop had ordained their father a deacon soon after he left Christ's College, Cambridge. At the very outset of his preaching they had imprisoned him at Northampton. When they released him, Marbury had immediately returned to the same place and the same kind of preaching, wherein he had criticized the appointment of unworthy ministers. Then they had called him before the High Commission. That was the part of the story that Anne loved! She never got over a leaping of the pulses whenever her father set the scene in Saint Paul's Consistory and rehearsed his defense before Bishop Aylmer. Stroke for stroke, the stubborn bishop and the equally stubborn young deacon hammered at each other's reasoning until they forgot reason and the bishop had called him "an overthwart, proud, Puritan knave," which Marbury had hotly denied. "Have him to the Marshalsea!" had cried the Bishop. The young deacon had answered boldly, "I am to go whither it pleaseth God, but remember God's judgments. You do me open wrong. I pray God to forgive you." So he went to prison again.

Thus would she speak, thought Anne, if she were a man! Not knowing that in such fashion she, a woman, would speak before another high tribunal.

She knew that a little later her father managed to secure the appointment to the living at Alford. Yet he could not stay out of trouble and, in 1590, he was again forbidden to preach. He at once wrote to Lord Burleigh, the High Treasurer of England, explaining that he had subscribed to the Communion Books and "did singularly mislike the inimes of sett prayer (enemies of set prayer)." They ignored his objections and they had compelled him to keep silent.

For fifteen years he had lived in Alford without preaching. He wrote "gentleman" after his name instead of "cleric," and kept his proud spirit and his slashing wit for his own household. He had a coat of arms and a little means, but Anne knew that he had never got over longing to write himself "cleric" again. Now he was restored.

Then came moving day in the Alford rectory. The last basket and cask and corded pack were ready for the wagoners. Carpets and hangings, thrum chairs, wrought stools and joint stools, oak coffers and trestle table, the one huge carved bed and many little pallets, the ever-needful cradle, the household plate and spinning wheels,

33

Holland Delftware and osier baskets — all Bridget Dryden's treasures were uprooted from the home of her bridehood and bound forth to make a new home as much like the old as possible.

Anne waited impatiently while her mother made her last sorrowful farewell trip over the house. Anne knew that her mother was saying good-bye to the room where her babies had been born and to the stairs they had tumbled down. She passed by the hearths that had warmed them and touched the thick timber and plaster walls that had housed them. She paused to gaze down the quiet street close by the gable end of the house, the green forecourt primly enclosed in its hedges, the sundial and the empty dovecotes. That was like her mother. As for Anne, her face was towards London.

What did the girl expect of London? She expected something fiercely, gloriously alive. Her conception of London came partly from what her father had told her, but more from the implicit attitude of everyone who spoke of London. She had heard little enough about the great writers of her day. No one yet knew that they were great. Besides, the name of Shakespeare or Ben Jonson would have meant loose merrymaking, playacting, and tavern drinking to Francis Marbury's sober household. The Puritan poet Milton was only a babe of three. Still, she had heard tales of English victories over Spaniards and wild Irishmen. She knew the names of Gilbert and Raleigh, of Frobisher, Drake, and Hawkins. A Lincolnshire girl, she could not fail to have heard her father talk intimately of friends who had sailed and fought and traded in foreign parts. She knew that the center of all this activity, the goal to which every adventurer brought treasures of experience, wealth, and curious lore, was London. In London there was a superb extravagance of living, denounced by the Puritans with equal extravagance of language. Sir Walter Raleigh, when they arrested him in 1603, was wearing four thousand pounds' worth of jewels.

They have said that Elizabethan England was "like a youth first come to the knowledge of his strength, rejoicing as a giant to run his course, and determined to do, to see, to know, to enjoy to the full." The whole country flamed into passionate life. Nothing was too hazardous or adventurous to attempt. Anne Marbury was born into Elizabethan England. Like the England of her girlhood, she had an unquenchable energy, spontaneity, enthusiasm, and was eager to meet life.

Still, to Anne, London meant mostly a place where her home was to be and where her father was going to preach. It meant a place where she would hear and see the famous ministers whose names had so often been on her father's lips. In those days a girl of fourteen was considered a young woman. Anne was "of a quick wit and ready mind," and was already expert in the controversial language of the day. She could give, with great promptitude, her opinion about the usages of the church, about the cross and the wedding ring, and whether it were better to kneel or not to kneel at the sacrament. A young gentlewoman like Anne could hardly expect or wish to go to the theater in London. However, she did look forward, with shuddering anticipation, to hearing the famous London preachers mow down their congregations with their terrifying eloquence. There would be rare treats in London!

Imagining the Marburys decked and girt for departure is easy. They stood in a little array of babies, bundles, adults and semi-adults, waiting for the carter's wagons to draw off and the coach to take its place. I should like to think that young Will Hutchinson appeared dressed in his Sunday best. He was wearing a short cloak of fine cloth over his shoulder and on his head a hat with a handsome buckle in it, the choicest of the stock in his father's shop.

"Will's got his best clothes on!" the children cry. "Will Hutchinson's going to London with us!"

However, Will has only come to say good-bye again and instead of saying it stands unhappily tongue-tied. The sight of him sets Anne to working faster among her brood, tying bonnets and pulling cloaks straight. So that at last he says drearily, "You are in great haste to be gone, Anne."

Anne laughs and says, "Who would not be in haste to go to London — unless he was fast asleep!" How odd for Will to make a ceremony of saying good-bye. Will Hutchinson whom she had led about by the nose ever since she was a baby and he a good, safe lad whom they could trust with little children. Now the high-headed girl of fourteen is almost as tall as the young man of nineteen. Her eyes, shining with elation, find themselves on a level with a pair that are full of pain. So she is sorry and gives him a kinder look.

The coach, old but dignified, bearing the Marbury arms "argent on a fess engrailed; gules three garbs of the first," draws up before the door. Francis Marbury marshals his family into their places within its too narrow limits. "Wife, make yourself comfortable, the journey is long. Now Susan! Now girls, Emmy, Biddy, in with you! Get in, you tadpoles, you Jerry and Dan! . . . Here, nurse, is a place for you and the babe. Anne — No! Erasmus, you ride in the coach. Anne goes pillion with me the first stage."

Erasmus draws down his mouth and holds back. Anne's eyes plead for him in spite of her first look of ecstasy.

In vain! "Tut, Erasmus, in with you! I said the first stage. Mother will need Anne's help more toward the journey's end. So in with you."

Erasmus crawls in and the ancient coach, filled to bursting, creaks off. John and Frank gallop alongside on one horse, while Erasmus glares at them from within. "Good-bye, Father — Good-bye, Anne," the boys shout. "We will see you at noon. Good-bye, Will."

Over the head of the eager Anne, her father looks searchingly into the troubled face of Will Hutchinson. "When your father sends you to London on his affairs, pray remember your old friends. God bless you, my lad. Put Anne on the pillion." He climbs to his horse and chides, "Anne, mind you are grown up now. Bid Will farewell graciously like a gentlewoman."

Slowly, with great care, Will Hutchinson lifts Anne to the pillion behind her father. Without being conscious of anything except that she is really starting, the young gentlewoman graciously gives her hand to her playmate the shopkeeper, and then, frankly kisses him. So they are off on the road to London. To London!

In spite of London, as Anne grew older, she would recall her old home. She would remember Will Hutchinson standing doleful and alone by the gate with his new buckled hat held reverently over his heart.

1.   Dryden, John (1631-1700). English poet, dramatist and critic. Dryden was the outstanding figure in letters during the Restoration and was literary dictator of his age.
       Dryden came from a good but impecunious country family with a

Parliamentarian and Church of England background. In his middle twenties, he went to London, where his gifts were quickly recognized in intellectual circles, though he had to struggle for years to earn a respectable living by means of his plays and translations. Dryden made several radical shifts in his religion and politics: in 1659 he eulogized Cromwell in the *Heroick Stanzas*; a year later, he celebrated Charles II in *Astraea Redux*; in 1682 he published RELIGIO LAICI, a defense of Anglicanism; five years later, THE HIND AND THE PANTHER revealed him as an ardent partisan of Catholicism and Catholic James II. In 1688, however, he refused to take an oath of allegiance to William and Mary, remaining loyal to James II at the cost of important offices, including the laureateship of England.

II

LONDON, 1605-1612

The energy that the Elizabethans put into fighting, writing, and exploring, the Jacobeans put into saving their souls. No play of Shakespeare's ever thrilled an audience more than the drama that the Puritans staged in their own minds over the struggle for their own souls. No setting could be more impressive than the heavens opening above them and the fires of hell roaring beneath their feet. As children, many of them had seen the old mystery plays in the streets and innyards. These performances had made the supernatural seem commonplace. Now, each earnest believer, weaving his personal drama, infused the commonplace events of his daily life with a supernatural significance.

Under James I, opposition began to intensify the zeal of those who longed to purify the English Church of its remnants of Popery. The story of the conference that the King had held with the leading Puritan clergy, a year and a half before, for the purpose of settling their differences was common knowledge. His Majesty called together the bishops and the ministers who wanted to root out the old forms, but it was a brief conference. No sooner had the clergy begun to stand out against the King and the bishops than the King became angry and dissolved the meeting. He threatened to make them conform, or harry them out of the land. Compulsion was the very thing that had been lacking to bring about a decided break. Such action was making avowed Puritans out of men who had formerly decried the name.

In the preceding reign, Queen Elizabeth had recognized the fact that three-fourths of the people were Puritan in temper. This included most of the country gentlemen, the tradespeople, and both Oxford and Cambridge Universities. She had been shrewd enough to bow outwardly to the majority, but James was more obstinate and far less politic.

So London, when Anne came there to live, was boiling with religious controversy. "Theology rules there," wrote the Dutch historian Grotius, describing England in that very year of 1605.

As Anne grew older, she heard matters of church form discussed at her father's dinner table. Marburys and Drydens, coming to London, called at the house of Francis Marbury. There may have come the Lentons, who were kinsmen of his mother, there may have come the kindred of his first wife, Elizabeth Moore. Among all these, as among the great bodies of the squirearchy throughout England, the talk ran to the ceremonials of their own church, the quality of their own ministers' preaching, and the state of their own souls. Clerical friends from the country made the Marbury rectory a convenient port of call. Other London clergymen often visited there. All these were trying to make up their own minds or convert the minds of others. Their debates focused on such matters of form as making the sign of the cross in baptism, kneeling at communion, or using sacred wafers. They argued the appropriateness of wearing copes, bowing at the name of Christ, and continuing the organ and the choir. They quarrelled about retaining the beautiful old stained glass windows, besides appointing ministers regularly educated and trained to preach.

Their religious opinions reflected many shades and degrees of difference. Puritan and near-Puritan, conformist, semi-conformist, and nonconformist, each had his own particular predilection. That of Francis Marbury happened to be for a properly trained clergy; it was a predilection that produced a fateful impression on the mind of his daughter Anne.

In spite of his Dryden connections, calling Marbury a Puritan is not accurate. Back in 1578, he indignantly denied the name when Bishop Aylmer in wrath tried to fit it to him. Again, in 1590, he wrote to Lord Burleigh that he had no sympathy with "those coming in at the postern door of supposed Puritanisme." He had had time enough since then to change his mind, but the fact that he got a church in 1605, under the sponsorship of Archbishop Bancroft, is quite good evidence that the Archbishop at least did not consider him a Puritan. His brother Edward had come into the possession of the Girsby estate over an older, disinherited brother Robert. He had so far won the favor of King James that he was knighted at Whitehall, July 23, 1603. The next year, he appointed Sir Edward Marbury Sheriff of Lincolnshire. Edward died that summer of 1605, but court favor stayed with his house, for his son George was knighted the next year. The influence of this honored family at Girsby may have helped Francis to obtain his appointment.

Bancroft himself owed his archbishopric to his advocacy of strict conformity. When they appointed him, he had a house-cleaning and, in the spring of 1605, swept out three hundred Puritan ministers. He had to replace these with more comfortable preachers and that was when Marbury, silenced for fifteen years, was restored.

Marbury's ordination, found in the Bishop of London's Registry, Liber Ordinationum, 1578-1628, reads as follows: "Francis Marbury, recently of Alford in the County and Diocese of Lincoln, but now of the City of London, aged forty-nine years or thereabouts, was ordained Deacon in the City of London (as he asserts) many years ago in the Borough of St. Peter by the Lord Edmund Scambler recently Bishop of Peterborough, and was now ordained Priest without testimonial because he is well-known to the Most Reverend the Archbishop aforesaid, and to the Lord Bishop of London aforesaid, and now was lawfully presented to the Rectory, to wit, of Martin in the Vintry of the City of London, vacant by the natural death of Master John Bateman, Clerk, the last Rector and Incumbent thereof."

The Archbishop and the Bishop mentioned were, respectively, Richard Bancroft of Canterbury and Richard Vaughan of London.

On the other hand, Anne's mother, if she took after the Dryden family, was a complete Puritan. Bridget's father, John Dryden, friend of the scholar Erasmus, in the preamble of his will bequeathed his soul to his Maker, "the Holy Ghost assuring my spirit that I am the Elect of God." Nothing could be more Calvinistic. Bridget's brother, Sir Erasmus Dryden, went to prison rather than lend money to King Charles I. Under the Commonwealth, his sons held government positions. John Dryden the poet, son of Bridget's nephew Erasmus (how proudly they reiterated that name!), was Puritan until it became convenient to change his religion with the Stuart

Restoration. Without doubt, Bridget Marbury brought Puritanism enough into the Marbury household.

At the Marbury table, Anne, with eyes and ears alert, might hear her Puritan Uncle Erasmus undertake to instruct some ritual-loving London clergyman in his duty. Her father frequently sounded the trumpet for his own particular *summum bonum,** an efficient preaching clergy. No one was persuaded except by his own opinions. Yet Anne, sitting fascinated on her stool, devoured the arguments and in time learned to take her part in the open and frank discussions of a critical family.

To this end she studied her little Geneva Bible more intensely. From babyhood they had brought her up to pore over it and to solve her problems by its light. The questions of church usages and government debated in her father's house seemed, to her, of profound consequence. She began to form opinions about them, which I am sure she managed to express. Gradually there developed in her a discriminating and difficult taste in preaching.

The London that Anne lived in seemed, to the country-bred girl, big enough to hold all the people in the world except the few that she remembered still living in

---

* Summum bonum (L.): the supreme good from which all others are derived.

Lincolnshire. The city really had a population of a hundred and fifty thousand and they crowded its narrow streets, though there were many open spaces. Anne, being the modest maiden daughter of a sober family, probably spent most of her time indoors, and saw very little of those crowded streets with their markets, playhouses, and bear gardens.* She got few glimpses of royal processions or court ladies in their Flemish coaches. She probably never visited the pleasure grounds along the Thames. It is likely she never saw the dockyards where velvets and glass from the Mediterranean, cloth from the Baltic, and spices from the East gave proof of England's supremacy on the sea. Shakespeare's *King Lear* and Ben Jonson's bitter *Volpone* were the new plays, though they meant nothing to Anne. Nevertheless, she heard about these things. The conversation at her university-bred father's table was not entirely about religion.

Anne heard talk of what was going on in the city. "The whole nation became a church," says the historian Green, but even preachers knew politics. The Marburys had hardly arrived when the Popish Plot was revealed. It made November 5, 1605, a day to be remembered in English history and increased the dread of popery in most

* Bear gardens: a place for bearbaiting and other rough pastimes.

English hearts. The next year Anne heard her father tell — his admiration mingled with disapproval — of the way the fiery Scotch preacher, Andrew Melville, had seized Archbishop Bancroft by the sleeves of his rochet, and shaken them, calling them popish rags and the mark of the beast. She heard that in Germany, the Emperor was trying to force his people to be Catholics. There were wars in Europe, with talk that she did not well understand about the Protestant Union and the Catholic League. She heard of proclamation after proclamation issued by King James. It must have seemed to her youthful mind that there were no laws except such as the King proclaimed from time to time. Perhaps she heard that James Stuart slobbered and staggered and told coarse jokes in broad Scotch. Nevertheless, she may have heard, too, that he was a scholar and no fool. She certainly heard that they were daily increasing the power of the Court of High Commission — a red rag[1] in Francis Marbury's house.

Anne's education was going on. By listening to the talk of her father and his friends, she got her instruction in current events. Looking from her leaded window over the steep, close-packed roofs of the city she realized her nearness to a great mass of humanity. By helping in the charities of the parish she gained experience and grew in sympathy. Though clinging vines did not come into fashion for a century and a half, most staid Jacobean citizens had no desire to see their womenfolk take part in public affairs. They did not yet approve boldness among women, unless one was a very grand lady indeed. Yet Anne, somehow or other, by the time she arrived at middle life had acquired a reputation for a "fierce and haughty carriage."

Life in London for Anne was not all religious discussions and strange sights. She still was her mother's lieutenant. She still had her duties in the nursery, which was never empty. Also, Anne was serving that apprenticeship in ministering to the sick that filled so important a place in her later life.

Two more Marbury babes were born during the London years, Anthony the second and Katherine. This second Anthony, named for the brother who had died in Alford, was born in 1608, evidenced by his matriculation entry at Oxford. Research did not uncover Katherine's birth date.

The care, and perhaps the rewards, of one living was not enough for Francis Marbury, now at last restored to his profession. On February 29, 1607, he was "presented to the Rectory" of Saint Pancras in Soper Lane. In a little while he resigned that incumbency and was appointed to Saint Margaret's in New Fish Street, January 15, 1609, while continuing with his offices at Saint Martin's. His Puritan colleagues probably accused him of "plurality," namely, of holding more than one living at a time, a practice that they condemned.

When Anne was nineteen and a half her father died. His death occurred in early February of 1611. So, after less than six years of parochial service in London, Francis Marbury, gentleman and cleric, fiery and banner-flaunting in youth, silenced and disappointed in early manhood, chastened and reconciled in his later years, was laid away in the peace of the church.

A few days later the Marburys gathered to hear the reading of their father's will. He had made it shortly before he died, for it bore the date of the preceding month, January 25.

The children sat with the widow Marbury in the rectory drawing room of Saint Martin's. The half-sister, Susan, then John, Anne, Francis, Erasmus, Jeremoth, Daniel, Emme, Bridget, Elizabeth, Anthony, and Katherine were the twelve living children.

The solicitor's grave voice droned out the details, after the usual preamble: "To each of my children, twelve in number, the sum of two hundred marks. To my eldest daughter Susan, an additional legacy of ten pounds. To my faithful maid servant, five marks. The rest of my estate

I do give and bequeath to my dear wife Bridget, she to keep all said children at her own charges one whole year after my decease if in the meantime she does not bestow them in marriage or place them in service. At the end of said year such children as are of age are to receive their portions, but can remain with their mother if they desire by paying her a proper allowance. The remaining children are to have their portions as they come of age and, if any of them die during their minority, their portion is to go absolutely to their mother. My wife Bridget Marbury to be sole executrix."

Mrs. Marbury recorded the will in the Consistory Court of London, one of the so-called "courts spiritual." The tiny fortune left by her husband was of more consequence than it would be now. The English mark was worth $3.23, which makes the legacies of the twelve children amount to about $8000, a sum that had a much greater purchasing power three-hundred-fifty years ago. Add to this the "rest of my estate" and one realizes that Francis Marbury must have been modestly comfortable.

After the father's death, the Marburys had to leave the rectory to make room for the new incumbent. They moved to a house somewhere in the combined parishes of Saint Mary Woolnoth and Saint Mary Woolchurch Haw. William Hutchinson, coming up from Alford on business to London, visited them there. He had probably done so at other times in the seven years since, buckled hat in hand, he had watched Anne ride away from Alford.

William was now a mature bachelor of twenty-six and he felt that it was high time he tried his luck with Anne. Nor was Anne of tender years. By the reckoning of the times, she was well on toward spinsterhood. Anne rewarded William's courage when he appealed to her on bended knee. Anne took her dowry of two hundred marks, her gentle blood, her unquenchable energy, and her enthusiasm and added them to the staid merchant stock of the Hutchinsons of Alford. In the register of the churches of Saint Mary Woolnoth and Saint Mary Woolchurch Haw was entered on August 9, 1612, the marriage of "William Hutchinson of Alford, County Lincoln, Mercer, and Anne, daughter of Francis Marbury, minister by license."

To his dying day, William Hutchinson was always a little in awe of his wife. He had no coat of arms, no manorial background like Canons Ashby or Girsby, and no university training. Nevertheless, he came of a family who had money in the till, a stout house to live in, and an honest name. His people were sound people. They had a capacity for personal loyalty. In later years, Will Hutchinson proved that the love of his wife meant more to him than the church or even personal comfort.

Anne's life was dedicated to the service of an ideal, illusive, preemptory, summoning her from one sacrifice to another. His was dedicated to the service of a woman and the children she bore him, and that dedication, too, compelled sacrifice.

"The genius of the family (the Hutchinsons) hath not much inclined to subtleties, scarce any of the Hutchinsons have been sectaries, unless *à latere,*[2] and indirectly," wrote the Reverend John Wheelright who married William Hutchinson's sister Mary.

Into a family that seems to have been normally more concerned with business than with religion, Anne brought a disturbing element.

1. Red rag: Something that arouses anger or vexation; from the phrase *like a red rag to a bull.*

2. À latere: to the earth.

III

THE HUTCHINSONS OF ALFORD

The Hutchinsons were self-made. It was a time in the history of England when the self-made man was beginning his laborious ascension. In part this was due to the general increase of England's commerce with the ports of the Old and the New World. Due in part also, to the enormous growth of one specific business, the wool industry.

The first Hutchinson to emerge from utter obscurity was William's great-grandfather. We do not know his first name, but it is certain that he lived in the shire town of Lincoln and that he had five children. One became a clergyman, another a man of property and honor — "alderman, tanner and glover" — and a third was energetic enough to climb from glover's apprentice to mayor of Lincoln. This was William's grandfather, John. One journalistic item has been handed down about Mayor John Hutchinson, to the effect that he died at four o'clock on a certain afternoon, and that within sixteen hours, his colleagues had attended his funeral and appointed his successor.

John left houses and lands to each of his five sons. The youngest of these, Edward, is the one who concerns us, for he was the father of Anne's husband. He was born about 1564, in Lincoln. After his apprenticeship to a mercer had expired, he moved to Alford, where he went into business and lived until his death in 1631.

Eleven children were born to Edward Hutchinson and his wife Susan. William was the eldest, born in 1586. The Hutchinsons had lived in Alford only one generation when Anne Marbury married into the family.

Of the brothers of William Hutchinson, we learn that Edward came to New England before William did and Samuel came later. John took up the lucrative business of woollen draper and married, as his second wife, Bridget Bury. Bridget, like our Anne, was a granddaughter of old John Dryden, Esquire, of Canons Ashby. Still another brother, Richard, became a wealthy citizen of London. He was an ironmonger and linen draper who made investments in American real estate and had the inestimable privilege of lending a large sum of money to his king. He lost sixty thousand pounds in the London Fire of 1666, without being ruined.

Concerning the Hutchinson sisters, it is recorded that Susan married Augustine Story, one of the grantees of

Piscataqua in New Hampshire. Mary became the wife of Reverend John Wheelwright whom they banished from Massachusetts in the controversy leading up to Anne Hutchinson's trial. He went to New Hampshire from Massachusetts.

The Hutchinsons of Alford were plain people. They were members of a class that was beginning to make itself felt in English life, but regarded by the gentry, great or small, as a cut beneath them. Good enough to borrow from and good additions to a business scheme like the establishment of a colony. Good enough to apprentice one's sons to — well enough to take into the family if one had a large flock of daughters to dispose of as Widow Marbury had. On August 9, 1612, Bridget Marbury saw her daughter Anne married to their former neighbor Will Hutchinson.

William and Anne went back to Alford and lived there twenty-two years. The parish register records the baptism of their first child Edward, named for his paternal grandfather, in May 1613. From that time, the William Hutchinsons appear in the baptismal records annually or biennially until November 1633. Fourteen, their children number on the parish rolls of Alford.

They buried three of the children in Alford. In 1630,

Anne lost two of her girls, Susan and Elizabeth. (Again, Elizabeth was an ill-omened name for the Marbury connection.) A little boy, William, born in June of 1623, died young, evidenced by the fact that William and Anne had another child christened by the same name in September of 1628.

This death toll was small in comparison with that of many families. It speaks well for the vitality of both parents and for the care that they took of their children. Parents in those days seemed to take the death of a child as a stroke of God, lamentable but beyond their power to avert. They grieved, but a new baby soon filled the place of the child they had lost, who often received the name of a dead brother or sister. One cause sometimes given for the high death rate among little children is the extreme youth of the parents. John Winthrop, first governor of Massachusetts Bay Colony, was twice a widower and seven times a father by the time he was twenty-seven. Girls usually married very young and often bore — and lost — three or four children before they were out of their teens. This was not the case with Anne. She was twenty-two when her first child was born. Her husband was twenty-seven. They were mature as couples went in those days.

What with babes and domestic tasks, the Hutchinson house in Alford must have been a busy place. Soap making and brewing, the endless preparation of cured meats, of lotions and cordials were some of the ordinary processes. For all this, Anne had plenty of servants. Times were hard, labor was cheap, servants were easy to find, and William Hutchinson's means were ample. Moreover, clothing took less thought than it does now. When they once wove cloth out of homespun linen or wool, it lasted. A woman's best dress not only served her for her own lifetime but was worth bequeathing to her daughter. Sheets and "pillow biers" were heirlooms. The same baby clothes sufficed for many little Hutchinsons. William, dealing in velvets, tamis* and good stout hollands,** picked out the best for his family. Anne saw to it that they made the fabric into garments that lasted.

Then, too, she taught each small Hutchinson daughter to perform her appointed household duty. Children of six in those days began to knit their own stockings. In an orderly Jacobean household, no one shirked assigned tasks. The constant supervision of this little commonwealth of twenty or more devolved upon Anne and helped to foster her natural ability as a manager.

---

* Tamis: a worsted cloth.

** Hollands: a kind of fine linen originally manufactured in Holland. It was sometimes glazed and used for children's clothing or upholstery.

Especially was it necessary that Anne should know how to look after the health of her household. The doctor might be hard to find and he was likely to be of small use if available. Every gentlewoman had, as part of her fundamental education, some training in the art of healing. A considerable part of this instruction was useful because it was based on practical experience; some of it sounds nothing short of deadly. In her family recipe books, Anne could find some possibly efficacious directions for dealing with common diseases. Appalling prescriptions for the plague, putrid fever, and the malady mysteriously described as the Evil had also been recorded there. As intelligent a man as John Winthrop, Jr., recommended for "agewes* of all sorts," that the healer pare the patient's nails and tie the parings around the neck of an eel in a tub of water. "The eel will die and the patient recover," he gravely concludes. Other directions were more practical, however, and the housewife knew of ways to relieve pain if not to cure. They taught her to dress wounds and to bind up arteries. She could even deal with a simple bone fracture.

Anne had learned the art of healing in her father's parish. In William Hutchinson's house — or is it more accurate to say in her own house? — she surely continued

---

* Agues: fevers.

the practice. We know from many accounts, in America she was wise in caring for the sick and gave herself unstintedly to all sorts of good works. It is not reasonable to suppose her character experienced a sea-change when she crossed the Atlantic and that in America she exhibited a taste and skill she had never shown at home. What she was in middle age is a sure indication of her pursuits while she was a younger woman in Alford.

In a seventeenth-century home like Anne's, the day began in the small hours when the mistress set her servants to work. They were all up and busy by five o'clock. By six, William's shop came to life. Not much later, the children were on their way to school, the little ones to dame school, the older boys to the grammar school. Eleven or twelve brought the adults of the family together for dinner. Gardening, sewing, and visiting the sick were the chores for the afternoon. The children returned at five from their long school day, had supper, and went directly to bed. The day ended as it began, with prayer and the reading of the Bible. Life was a sober affair, but it would have been peaceful and free from spectacular events, had not Anne been set astir by the religious excitement in the air.

While Anne lived in Alford, three of her brothers, Erasmus, Jeremoth, and Anthony, went to college. They chose Brasenose in Oxford, though why they did when their father had been a Cambridge man is hard to tell. Both universities in Queen Elizabeth's time had been hotbeds of Puritanism. However, by 1616, when the first of the Marbury lads matriculated, Oxford was showing a more obedient spirit. Erasmus Marbury, true to the name that he had inherited from the Dutch scholar, got his Master's degree and became a Fellow of his college. He died seven years before his sister Anne went to America.

Respected and prosperous, Anne Hutchinson and her good William might have followed the Hutchinson example and placidly continued to fill their house with children and their treasury with money in the quiet surroundings of an English market town. However, three disturbing forces worked together to upset the Alford home — the religious ferment of the time, the restlessness and vehemence of Anne's disposition, and the personality of the preacher of Saint Botolph's in Boston.

IV

THE FIRST STEP

Almost as soon as Anne and her husband became settled in their Alford home, rumors came flying about the countryside concerning the eloquence and learning of a young preacher in Boston, twenty-four miles away.

The new preacher, who was destined to exert the greatest influence over Anne and the fortunes of her family, was John Cotton. For twenty-one years, Cotton was Vicar of Saint Botolph's in old Boston. For nearly twenty years more, he was the teacher of the first church in the new Boston of America.

It was in the summer of Anne's bridehood that the Corporation of old Boston appointed Cotton to the vicarate of Saint Botolph's. The appointment came almost by chance. Cotton's remarkable work as "head-lecturer, dean and catechist" at Emmanuel College, Cambridge, had attracted the favorable attention of the Puritans in the Corporation. Nevertheless, the prestige of Bishop Barlow of Lincoln reenforced an adverse party. The first ballot was a tie and, only by an error, was Cotton elected.

Somehow, the mayor became confused and cast his vote, not once but twice for Cotton, when he thought he was voting the other way. If the mayor had not blundered — and if Cotton's supporters had not used something very much like bribery with one of Bishop Barlow's agents — they would have much altered the whole history of Anne Hutchinson's life.

At first, it is likely that Anne was too closely occupied with her home to pay much attention to the reports of Mr. Cotton's preaching. However, it could not have been long before he aroused her curiosity. Anne was always a keen student of the Bible and they had brought her up in an atmosphere of theological discussion. What she heard of the Boston vicar promised her the intellectual and spiritual food she craved in her rural home.

"Take me to Saint Botolph's to hear this new preacher," we can hear her demanding. William, eager to please, would agree. The trip was surely a frequent occurrence for a businessman like William and he had many connections in Boston. So, we may imagine Anne riding on a pillion behind her husband, bound to spend the weekend in Boston.

They rode through the soft misty light of spring, the lush greenness of summer, the wood-smoke and brown fields of autumn. Olive green willows lined still streams full to the banks, thatched roofs blended with thick trees, tiny villages hid themselves in the recesses of Lincoln Wold. William followed Boston Stump as a guide until they reached the picturesque marketplace of Boston. Then they rode along the placid river Witham, from whose bank rose sheer the most wonderful parish church in all England.

They spent many hours in the church itself. It was so comfortable and so simple. Yet, it was so curiously contrived with seven doors, twelve pillars in the nave, twenty-four steps to the library, sixty to the chancel roof, and three hundred sixty-five steps to the tower.

Then, off and on for years, Anne Hutchinson sat with her husband's kindred Sunday mornings in the glorious old church. She listened to the insinuating and melting discourse of the Vicar and felt that here indeed was the preaching for which her soul had hungered. He preached Sunday afternoons and, again, she hastened to the meetings. In the mornings, his preaching was "experiential and pastoral," teaching from the Scriptures the way to live a good life. In the afternoons, it was theological. Both were manna to Anne Hutchinson, but always the former seemed to her of more consequence than the latter. The communion of her spirit with the spirit of God meant more to her than doctrine. By the spirit, she lived.

There were Thursday lectures, too. Mr. Cotton

"preached through the whole First and Second Epistles of John, the whole book of Solomon's Song, [and] the Parables of our Saviour." Besides that, if Anne happened to be in Boston Wednesday or Friday mornings, or Saturday afternoons, she could hear the Vicar give a kind of informal talk. The performances at Saint Botolph's were nearly continuous. This was the Puritan's conception of a minister's job. Even the more comfortable Francis Marbury had some such ideal when he talked about "the true ministry." This standard of preaching he had passed on to his daughter.

During this period — perhaps in 1616-17, inasmuch as they gave the name Faith to the baby born that year — Anne went through a period of intense mental and spiritual conflict. In later years she rehearsed it and they fortunately recorded her words, though by no friendly hand. "Being much troubled in those days to see the falseness of the constitution of the Church of England," she affirmed, "I had like to have turned Separatist."

To turn Separatist was a hard thing. It meant withdrawing from the church of her fathers, the church with which she had indissolubly connected much of her life. It meant allying herself with men and women who were of humble birth, poorly educated, and essentially under the stigma of fanaticism.

They had treated the Separatists roughly in Lincolnshire. In 1607, while Anne was living in London, the Scrooby congregation from the border of Northampton-shire and York had tried, under the leadership of John Robinson and William Brewster, to leave the country. In England, they were "a byword, a mocking-stock, and a matter of reproach," and they sought refuge in Holland. They had come to Boston, where they expected to get a boat for the Dutch country. However, they had been betrayed to the customs officials, tried in Saint Mary's Guildhall and confined for a month in the vaults below. Then they were returned to their homes. They did not give up, but tried again, and the next year got across to Holland. Seven hundred more followed in 1609. This happened before Anne's marriage. Still, the remembrance of it was fresh in the minds of those in the neighborhood who had seen the poor Separatists made a "spectacle and a wonder to the multitude." Those Separatists who remained kept quiet. They had to worship in private houses and out-of-the-way places, in unorganized, undisciplined convocations. Anne liked to be up and doing, openly and in company with others, too much to choose Separatism unless conscience forbade any other way. For a whole year she labored with her trouble.

Finally, her mind and spirit in agony, Anne kept a day

of solemn humiliation in the hope of coming to a decision. The work of the house had to go on, but it went softly, as if sickness was there. The maid servants stole quietly about, for the mistress was above the stairs, shut in her room since early morning. They hushed the babes. If it were really in 1616, there were three tiny Hutchinsons — Edward, Susan, and Richard. Three-year-old Edward alone was old enough to realize that they must not disturb their mother. The master ate his meal hastily and departed as from a house of mourning. Still Anne wrestled with her problem. Without food and without rest, behind her closed door she sought guidance from her Bible.

Fasting and concentration, she afterwards affirmed, brought her mind to rest upon the Second Epistle of John 1:7 — "He that denies Jesus Christ is come in the flesh is a deceiver and antichrist."

What did that mean? Why did that sentence tease her tortured mind? Who was it that denied Him to be come in the flesh? Not the Church of England, not the Papists. Both these admitted His coming. Then who was antichrist? Was it none but the Moslem Turk alone?

She prayed the Lord to show her, for He knew that she could not interpret Scripture by herself. "Show me. I pray Thee!" she implored. "Rend the veil that hides Thy truth from me!"

Again her mind rested on a passage, this time Hebrews 9:16. "He that denies the testament denies the testator." Then he who denies Christ is he who denies the testament that is the new covenant. For the Scripture says in Hebrews 8:6, "Now hath He obtained a more excellent ministry, by how much more also He is the mediator of a better covenant, which was established upon better promises."

The obscure phrases yielded light as she agonized over them. When describing this crisis in later years, she said, "So it came to me that he is antichrist who doth not teach the new covenant. The new covenant is that which rests wholly upon the word of God as given in the Bible, and not on ordinances, forms, and ceremonies imposed by man." In other words, she had become a nonconformist, rebelling against the ceremonies enjoined by the bishops, and once so loved. It now became clear to her that she had no need to turn Separatist. The true doctrine could be found within the church, in the mouths of preachers who sought to purify it of forms established by man. Now was her groaning turned to joy. In place of supplication she gave thanks that she could distinguish between the voice of Christ and the voice of Moses, the voice of John the Evangel and the voice of antichrist. In other words, she could now tell the difference between those who preached Christ alone and those who added rites and ceremonies. She praised God for her ability to discriminate and pass judgement.

The mistress descended from her chamber and the house smiled again. However, the decision she had made was portentous and affected the lives of them all. She was now positively and consciously a nonconformist.

"Since that time," she avowed later, "I confess I have been more choice. I bless the Lord that He hath let me see which was the clear ministry and which was the wrong. Ever since that time, I have been confident of what He revealed to me." This crisis, therefore, marked the beginning of her conviction that God spoke to her directly out of His Word, that her decisions and her distinctions were inspired.

Francis Marbury's daughter was now willing to come out boldly for what she considered the clear ministry. Of this clear ministry, John Cotton was to her the bright and shining light. Under his leadership Saint Botolph's had become a religious center. Men and women from all over England consulted him in person or by writing about matters of conscience. Anne gave herself unreservedly and enthusiastically to his guidance.

Cotton had been at Saint Botolph's about three years when a sensitive listener like Anne must have detected a change in his attitude toward the use of the Prayer Book.

He had always been a Puritan in his way of living. By 1615, he became convinced that it was "utterly unlawfull for any church power to enjoyn the observation of ceremonies which Christ had not commanded." Being an occasional visitor, Anne could see the gradual changes in the services at Saint Botolph's more clearly than a regular attendant, for they came by minute degrees. Little by little, as the years went by, Cotton simplified the service. He gave up wearing the surplice, he no longer used the cross in baptism, he did not require communicants to kneel at the sacrament. All these practices Anne had seen her father observe, for Francis Marbury had conformed so far as rites went. His rock of offense had been a better kind of clergy — "the clear ministry." Those words became a battle cry to his daughter, but she meant more by them than he did.

As late as 1624, they were still observing the liturgy of the Prayer Book in the ordinary church services at Saint Botolph's. However, there was a kind of inner circle of true seekers, "some scores of godly persons in Boston who entered into a Covenant with the Lord and with one another to follow the Lord after the purity of His worship." Anne Hutchinson, though hampered by distance, belonged in spirit to this exclusive group.

Cotton's gradual innovations in his church did not

escape opposition. They made the first attacks on some of his adherents who held church office.

For example, consider the case of Mr. Atherton Hough, he was later a Hutchinson man in new Boston. Hough was a church warden in old Boston in Cotton's time and got into trouble by following his vicar's leading. On February 16, 1622, the case of Thomas Shaw of Boston, gentleman, against Atherton Hough and others was tried in the Star Chamber. Shaw accused Hough of destroying and removing the stained glass windows of the church. They also charged him with conveying away the ornamental cover of the font surmounted with that curiously carved dove, and setting up in its place "a piece of blackwood in likeness of a pott lid." They also accused Hough, Edmund Jackson and "divers sectaryes" of removing the cross from the mace that the mayor carried in processions to the church. We must remember that old ways were very dear to many Englishmen. The irony of it was that both Puritans and non-Puritans accused each other of being newfangled.

To the joy of the Puritan element, Anne included, they dismissed Hough on the plea that all the things of which they accused him concerning the windows and the font happened before he came to the church. As for removing the cross from the mace, they had already heard and dismissed that in a lower court.

As the years passed, the cleavage between the conformists and the nonconformists of Saint Botolph's became more evident and ecclesiastical control was tightened. In 1632, they made complaint to the Court of High Commission that Cotton did not make the magistrates kneel when they took Communion and that he neglected other regulations of the Court. Not even Cotton's good friend, the Earl of Dorset, who had helped him out of difficulty before, could do better this time than advise flight. The charge was "not a simple thing like drunkenness, uncleanness or any lesser fault," but nonconformity.

Three courses were open to Cotton: he could stop preaching, conform, or leave England. He chose to leave. After wavering between Holland, the Barbados, and New England, he decided upon the last. He had good friends there. He had preached the farewell sermon when John Winthrop and his party set sail from Southampton for America in the spring of 1630. With dignity and nobility of phrasing, he wrote a letter of resignation to the new bishop of Lincoln. Cotton was on better terms with Bishop Williams than with old Bishop Barlow. Then, with some difficulty, he got out of England. On September 4, 1633, he arrived in Boston in New England by the ship Griffin.

At the going of John Cotton, Anne Hutchinson's heart

quailed. No other port or haven in all England has so high a beacon as the lantern on the great tower of Saint Botolph's. Likewise, to Anne's ardent soul no other preacher in all the country was so lofty a guide. Under his leadership she had come to her present state of assurance and now they had put down her guide. She had surrounded him with the halo that a devoted feminine listener can so readily create for a beloved preacher. This had its effect. Cotton, on his part, was acquainted with Mrs. Hutchinson's reputation for good works. He knew the Hutchinsons for a substantial family with means fitted to carry out her charitable inclinations. He would have been more than human if the frank admiration of this discriminating, high-minded and capable gentlewoman had not gratified him. Now he was gone and she was bereft.

The treatment accorded her brother-in-law, John Wheelwright, further increased Anne's own dissatisfaction with the state of the clergy in her neighborhood. It was Wheelwright who had married for his second wife Mary, sister of William Hutchinson. His nonconforming zeal had attracted unfavorable attention. By 1633, they had silenced him on a technical charge of selling his vicarate and his living at Bilsby declared vacant. He was now preaching privately, to the great edification of the faithful, but under the ban of the law. Wheelwright and Cotton were the only preachers who seemed to Anne to belong to the "clear ministry." They had silenced one of them, the other, far dearer, had been forced out of England. How was she to meet that intolerable situation?

Cotton's successor at Saint Botolph's was a worthy man, but too conforming for Anne's delicate perceptions, and he was not John Cotton. As for the preaching in her own home church, it evidently seemed negligible, for she does not even refer to it in her account of her spiritual famine.

It was no fiction of the Puritans that the country churches were shockingly ill supplied. Richard Baxter, writing of that period in his autobiography, says that four "readers" in six years served the church in his village. "Ignorant men, and two of them immoral in their lives." He continued, "There was a reader of some eighty years old who never preached and had two churches about twenty miles distant. His eyesight failing him, he said Common Prayer without the book. But for the reading of the Psalms and Chapters he got a common thresher and day-laborer one year, and a tailor another year." He also wrote, "And at last he had a kinsman of his own (the excellintist stage-player in all the country and a good gamester and a good fellow) that got orders and supplied one of his places.

After him another younger kinsman, who could read and write, got Orders. At the same time another neighbor's son, who had been a while at school, turned minister, one who would needs go further than the rest, and ventured to preach. When he had been a preacher about ten years, he was fain to give over, it being discovered that his orders were forged by the first ingenious stage-player."

Conditions among the rural clergy had not improved since the time when hotheaded young Francis Marbury stormed at Bishop Aylmer for having appointed ministers unable to preach.

In 1633, Laud, the clothier's son, became head of the English Church. He brought the whole subject of conformity to a sudden issue, summoning, silencing, or removing hundreds of Puritan ministers. That same year, John Milton, destined for orders, wrote, "Perceiving what tyranny had invaded the church, that he who would take orders must subscribe, slave, and take an oath withal, which unless he took with a conscience that would stretch, he must either straight perjure or split his faith, I thought it better to prefer a blameless silence before the sacred office of speaking, bought and begun with servitude and foreswearing."

It was not for lack of occupation that Anne

Hutchinson's mind and heart were so set on the matter of right preaching. Throughout these twenty years of spiritual quest, she had continued to augment the number of His Majesty's subjects at the average rate of one every seventeen months. Nevertheless, her vitality did not become impoverished. She had enough for her family and much besides — but she could not endure without spiritual food. Actually, she had reached a point in her spiritual development where she could have been a minister, an inspired one, who could feed a flock. But females were banned from the pulpit. That advance had to wait two hundred more years.

V

THE FIRST REMOVAL

No one in all England whose preaching she could endure!

To a woman like Anne Hutchinson this was devastating. We can compare her deprivation with that of an alert and cultivated woman of the twentieth century being deprived of books, music, the theater, lectures, and the conversation of her equals. It meant losing romance and losing her way of escape. Called by any name, Cotton's going meant severance with that whereby her spirit lived. The desert looked all the more drear because she saw herself left, not only without an intellectual stimulant on earth, but without the means of salvation hereafter. Looking back on this period five years later in New England, she declared, "When our teacher John Cotton came to New England it was a great trouble to me, my brother Wheelwright being put by also. I was then much troubled concerning the ministry under which I lived. . . . I could not be at rest but I must come hither."

A psychoanalyst might aver that Anne Hutchinson loved religion in the form of her preacher, or that she loved her preacher under the guise of religion. To her they were identical; she did not separate one from the other. What she really loved and sought was an outlet for her tremendous energy. She spoke truly when she said she could not be at rest until she removed. The good William, her huge family, her neighborhood benevolences were not enough. Preachers and preaching, human friendship and religion, ambition for her children, and a genuine fear for the future of England were inextricably involved with a passionate desire for a change. She longed to be up and away and doing something different.

As usual, Anne turned to her Bible for guidance — after the unconscious wish had established itself. She did not find guidance at once, not the kind she was seeking. At times she withdrew from her family, hunting for light in the pages of the Holy Book. At other times she went swiftly and competently about her tasks, but with her mind abstracted from her work. The emptiness possessed Anne, the appalling prospect of spiritual starvation stretched before her.

She had shut herself off from all the spiritual communion available. Anne was determined not to conform to the usages prescribed for the established churches and, simultaneously, not to join the clandestine meetings of the despised Separatists. As she had grown to mature womanhood, her natural tendency to mysticism, fostered by the atmosphere of her father's house and the example of her mother's family, had gained head. She must pursue the way of God; she could not have a moment's comfort if she suspected that she was deviating from it. If she had to choose between food for her body and food for her soul, she would choose the latter. Moreover, she was too vividly alive not to put her mysticism into practice. Not content merely to meditate upon God's ineffable wisdom and glory, she had to translate her meditations into prompt, even drastic action, for herself and for others.

So, when they took her preachers away from her, she had to do something about it. The first needful thing was to find authority for her own course. Secondly, Anne had to swing her family into line. The first was by far the harder to do, but help must come from the Word. She recognized no other authority.

Here we can turn to the very words in which she afterwards described this decisive moment. "I was then much troubled concerning the ministry under which I lived, and then that place in the thirtieth of Isaiah [30:20] was brought to my mind. 'Though the Lord give you the bread of adversity, and the water of affliction, yet shall not thy teachers be removed into a corner anymore, but thine eyes shall see thy teachers.'"

Here was a passage from Holy Writ surely brought to her eye by direct intention in answer to her prayer. God thus showed His personal interest in her. He spoke to her out of His Word, to her, Anne Hutchinson of Alford in England. Therefore, she was under compulsion to pore over that passage and wrest from it its hidden, personal message. It contained her orders. They were written in a cipher, but it would be eternally fatal if she should fail to understand them. So she bent her mind to finding out the key to the cipher. She thanked God that she had a mind. Anne believed in her ultimate ability to interpret the passage and apply it to her immediate problem.

"Thy teachers shall not be removed into a corner anymore." What did that mean? They certainly had been removed. John Cotton was gone; John Wheelwright was forbidden to preach. Did it mean there were other teachers whom she could trust? Ah, she very well knew that she could not endure any of them. (Here the personal element entered into her interpretation of God's orders.)

"But thine eyes shall see thy teachers" — that must mean that she was to be where her teachers were. John Cotton was in New England. Was that the answer? Did it mean she was to follow Cotton to New England? Might it not mean that?

She did not need the warning, "Though the Lord give you the bread of adversity, and the water of affliction." Superficially, going would not be easy. It meant giving up her home, leaving friends, exchanging the accustomed ways of England for the horrors of an ocean voyage and the harshness of a new continent. She looked regretfully about her comfortable chamber. Anne prayed. She held her heart still and waited for the Lord to speak.

Her Lord spoke. Out of His Word she read from Daniel 6:27 — "He delivereth and rescueth, and He worketh signs and wonders in heaven and in earth, Who hath delivered Daniel from the power of the lions."

He Who had delivered Daniel would deliver Anne Hutchinson. Even though she should be made to eat the bread of adversity and drink the water of affliction. Even though she should offer that bread and that water to her husband and children. The path was perfectly plain. All that remained was for her to lead her husband and children in it.

A glow of adventurous longing grew and spread until it warmed her whole being. Anne was feeling the exaltation of doing a hard thing for conscience' sake. The thought of doing something momentous, difficult, and sure to cause comment among her neighbors created an undeniable excitement. Psychologists observing Anne

Hutchinson's behavior with the disillusioned eyes of the twentieth century may murmur something about "exhibitionism." But women seldom try to show off before their own husbands. Anne's husband was the first person to whom she must carry the news of her decision. William was well trained to her direction, but this time she was asking something that would turn his world upside down. It made her task much easier, she gladly realized, that their eldest son Edward, together with William's brother Edward, had already gone to America, in company with John Cotton.

Anne's spiritual turmoil had not passed entirely unnoticed by her husband. While she prayed and wrestled with her Bible, even William knew that something was wrong. Her sharp unrest caused a nervous tension. She did not neglect her family, yet she did not make them happy. She was as swift, as mechanically capable, but she was propelled upon her tasks like one tormented. Her husband, whose love was made up of a kind of awed worship and a yearning to serve her, felt thwarted and apprehensive. In an unformulated way he braced himself for some kind of upheaval. The upheaval came in the spring of 1634.

The time had arrived when Anne must tell William

what was on her mind. Imagine a day, perhaps a Sunday, when there was leisure for a prolonged conference. The late afternoon sun shone through the diamond paned windows of the great chamber in William Hutchinson's house. It was a sweet afternoon, fragrant with sprouting gardens, not the kind of day or season when one would wish to leave England. In and about the house, the children were yawning over the confinement of Sunday in a Puritan household. They were gazing after their freer comrades going gaily to the green or to the fields. The young Hutchinsons' sense of superior virtue could only partly assuage their longing to be free.

In the chamber above, sat the father and mother in council. They were middle-aged. She was close upon forty-three; he was five years older. Their most active years were running short. Full of responsibilities but respected and prosperous, they could look forward to a period of peace. William's father had died three years before and William had, for some time, been sole proprietor of the business. There was nothing momentous to worry him, nothing more than the exacting but customary problems of settling his big family of boys and girls. *Nothing else to worry him except his wife!*

Their words have not been recorded. However, it would be like Anne to begin sensibly enough, speaking of their own kin. She would talk about their boy Edward over in America, the boy's Uncle Edward who was there with him, and about John Wheelwright, husband of William's sister Mary.

"It will not be long, you may mark my words, before John Wheelwright follows Mr. Cotton to America. What comfort is there for him, preaching privately, in fear of the law? He would do well to ask Brother Edward to see what opportunity there is for him across the water."

"Perhaps," William replied without enthusiasm. "Poor Mary!"

"Poor Mary? Nay!" his wife flashed. "What better place in which to bring up a family than in a rich new country? Did you say 'Poor Sarah' when Brother Edward took her to New England? Did you forbid your own son to go?"

"Edward *would* go," said Edward's father.

"And in that he chose well," said Edward's mother firmly. "Look at the men who have gone and are going with every ship — men of judgement and property. Mr. William Coddington thinks so well of New England that he stayed here long enough only to find a new wife and back he went. Atherton Hough, Edmund Quincy, John Leverett, you knew them all at Saint Botolph's parish for sound men."

"Ay, sound men enough," William granted, "but a cursed thing to leave their affairs behind them."

"There is Thomas Dudley, too," his wife went on, undeterred. "He is a Lincolnshire man and was steward to the old Earl. I have been told that he is now one of the chief men in the colony. They say that by summer Mr. John Humphrey and the Lady Susan will have gone. If a woman who is a daughter of one Earl of Lincoln and sister of another can endure the change, what need to say 'Poor Mary'?"

"I would say poor Lady Susan if she fare no better than her sister, Lady Arbella. Dying as soon as she reached New England, and her husband not long after. When I die, I would sooner feed the worms in Alford churchyard," said William.

"When you die," retorted his wife, "it will make no difference to you whether your mortal body feeds the worms of Old England or New England. Those who crossed the ocean went for conscience' sake and count their tribulation for glory."

"Ay," said William shrewdly, "and many of them have money invested in the Massachusetts Company."

Anne passed over her husband's implication. "They have true preaching in the colony, so that if their bodies endure hardship, their souls rejoice. Since Mr. Cotton has gone, you must know that I have starved."

Yes, William knew; he also knew that not all his affection could heal her loss.

She bent her fine brows sorrowfully. "I grieve for our children and fear for them that they must grow up without the light. Better to walk in the light in a strange place than to dwell in darkness at home. Besides," her tone grew brisk, "in New England there are good chances for young men. Is not land to be had for the asking? Are there not shops to be kept and products to be traded to England? And room for each man his own estate? What can old England give our children that the New World does not overmatch a hundred times?"

William sat folded in thought. There was something in what she said; there always was.

"And young men to marry our daughters," his wife went on, "and our dear friend to preach to us again, and God's law the law of the land!" She leaned forward and laid her clasped hands upon her husband's while she repeated solemnly, "'Though the Lord give you the bread of adversity, and the water of affliction, yet shall not thy teachers be removed into a corner anymore, but thine eyes shall see thy teachers.' And He Who delivered Daniel from the power of the lions, He will deliver thee."

William felt his resolution wavering. He knew the

passages she had quoted, each one from a prophetic book of the Old Testament, but was Anne sure the words were meant for them? Hopelessly he gathered himself for a last show of resistance.

Anne was sure. What better proof than that her eye had been unmistakably guided to those very pages and verses? William's slow mind could not leap the Atlantic so quickly. To leave his birthplace, his friends, to uproot his family and his business, to make a fresh start at forty-eight! To pack up and leave Alford, to get aboard a vessel with King's officers raising all sorts of hard questions, to find a home for his family and make a living, all for the sake of "seeing their teachers!" *All for the sake of making Anne happy.* That was another matter.

Ay, William admired Mr. Cotton hugely. Himself, he was no person to split hairs and get excited over doctrine. He wanted to do what was right, owe no man anything, provide for his family. And please his wife. *Yes, please his wife.*

There were good chances in America. Great lords were behind this New England project — the Earl of Warwick, Lord Say and Sele, Lord Brook, their own Earl of Lincoln. All a man needed in the new country, he had heard, was a little money to begin with, a little courage — Anne had enough of that — a little business sense — he hoped he had that. The two Edwards seemed to be sticking — at least they had not got home yet.

And Anne said she could not be happy in England. If she said it was God's will that they should go, he knew what that meant. Still, pray God they got a bad report from the Edwards before they started!

Anne, however, had made up her mind to go, and the question was closed.

If the decisive conversation between husband and wife took place in such words as these, it was consistent with the character of each, for always Anne led and William followed. In some manner, on some spring day in 1634, the choice was made that became "the cause of more fomentation in New England" than anything that had happened there before.

VI

IN FOUR-YEAR-OLD BOSTON

The Hutchinsons set sail for America in the summer of 1634, on the same vessel that had, the year before, brought John Cotton. They felt the safer because the good ship Griffin had proved a safe carrier for so many of their friends. She was of three hundred tons burden and could accommodate about two hundred passengers. However, on this trip, the Griffin and her companion ship together brought only two hundred. With them came a hundred head of cattle that John Winthrop had asked to have sent over.

The Hutchinsons survived the ordeal of the King's searchers who came aboard before the ship could sail. They demanded to see the lists of passengers, gave the oath of allegiance, viewed the necessary certificates from each emigrant's parish minister, and issued passports. Anne managed to enjoy some hours of her trip across the Atlantic. Talking was always one of her chief pleasures and we have record that she talked, too much indeed for her own good. It may not have been the first time that she did so; certainly, it was not the last. It was in the tradition of the impetuous Marburys to open their mouths to their own hurt.

The trip was inconvenient enough, with the passengers in painful proximity to Winthrop's cattle.[1] However, no one expected to be comfortable. They strengthened themselves against their vexations by holding prayer and experience meetings. They listened to the daily preaching and exposition of the Reverend Zachariah Symmes and the Reverend John Lothrop. The captain, if he were a Puritan, would even set the watches to the tune of a psalm and extemporaneous prayer. In the intervals between worship there was always plenty of edifying conversation about the state of England and of their own souls. We may suppose that they also discussed their prospects in the new country, though such worldly discourse was not considered worth recording.

In spite of the cramped quarters, all on board had a blessed sense of freedom and exhilaration. They could express their views frankly and enjoy the unhampered communion of kindred minds. They had started out with a whole day of preaching, praying and fasting. The latter holy exercise was in no wise objectionable to those now going to sea for the first time in their lives. The whole long trip — it usually took from fifty to seventy days, though occasionally the passage was made in less time — was one glorious, protracted meeting. It was doubly delightful because they had never before had quite enough of that kind of freedom. They still perceived in it the sweet flavor of a proceeding frowned upon by the authorities at home. It was an excellent initiation into New England ways for the ungodly who were on board. There were always more of those than is commonly supposed.

Among the whole company, no one talked more brilliantly than Anne Hutchinson or expressed more positive convictions. She soon found herself the center of a little court who stimulated her quick tongue to voice whatever her swift mind conceived.

However, every court has its malcontents. In the time between leaving Alford and taking ship, the Hutchinsons had stayed in London at the house of William Bartholomew, who was to be their fellow traveler. Mr. Bartholomew afterwards recalled that, though Anne Hutchinson disclosed no startling ideas in his house, she did once while walking with him through Saint Paul's churchyard. She became "very inquisitive after revelations and said that she never had any great thing happen to her but it was revealed to her beforehand." The Reverend Mr. Symmes also fell foul of her even before they started, while they were waiting for their vessel to make ready. Her spacious utterances roused suspicions in his unequivocal mind and he began thus early to doubt the soundness of her doctrine.

One day on shipboard, in the innocent elation of her great adventure, she made the same disclosure that she had made to William Bartholomew. Anne repeated, "Nothing great ever befell me that was not made known to me beforehand." Mr. Symmes was shocked. He did not believe that the Almighty thus admitted poor human beings to His confidence.

Here was the germ of a debate and Anne hastened to nourish it. Others gathered around — among them Bartholomew and the Reverend John Lothrop. Anne maintained her opinion vigorously. "Remember you not," she said, "what so learned a divine as the Reverend Thomas Hooker said? In public meeting he admitted that he received revelations of events that were to occur in the future. Mr. Hooker's spirit, I like not," she acknowledged with her customary frank discrimination. "But I was pleased with a sentence in a sermon that he preached just before leaving England, when he said that it had been revealed to him the day before that England should be destroyed."

She caught her eight-months-old babe to her breast and lifted her glowing eyes to the unresponsive face of Mr. Symmes. "Do you think I would expose my little ones to the wilderness without some great cause? My heart would have fainted at the thought of bringing my children to a strange land if I, too, had not received revelation of a worse fate if they remained in England. I, too, have been warned that for her sins that unhappy land shall be plucked up by the roots and cast forth."

Her family was evidently greatly impressed with her prophetic power. Honest William appears to have given it out that his wife had foretold the very day when they should come to land. Her eldest daughter, Faith, catching the mode of speech from her mother, avowed that she also had a revelation. She said that a certain young man on board would be saved, but that in order to do so he must first walk in the way of her mother.

All this severely tried the patience of Zachariah Symmes. "Strange opinions!" he said morosely when he and William Bartholomew were out of the lady's hearing. "And very freely vented!" agreed the other. Later, whenever Anne Hutchinson discoursed eloquently to the circle of her listeners, who grew more numerous as the voyage continued, Mr. Symmes sat disapproving and aloof. When he arrived in Boston, one of his first duties was to warn the church not to admit the wife of William Hutchinson to membership until they had held her for a time under observation. Mr. Bartholomew, too, laid up her innocent and spontaneous words against her and recalled them four years later when she stood on trial before the General Court. John Lothrop was too gentle a man to condemn her and, perhaps, his long imprisonment in England for conscience' sake had rendered him more charitable. Nevertheless, he admitted that he shared privately the feeling of his brother-minister Symmes.

The intellectual and spiritual fare on board the Griffin was better than the physical. It was, in dead earnest, a place of high thinking and plain living. Transportation cost William Hutchinson five pounds apiece for himself and wife, with varying reductions for the children according to age. His goods were carried at the rate of four pounds a ton. Salt meat and hard bread, varied by oatmeal, pease porridge, and salt fish, formed the principal diet on board, and one particularly unsuitable for children. Beer was the usual beverage. When they took water, it was well dashed with malaga or canary.* Passengers were advised to take a store of lemons, but not all were able to follow the advice. No wonder many children died of scurvy at sea in those days. The mother of a big family of boys and girls ranging from maturity to infancy must have sung a song of thanksgiving when at last the

---

* Malaga and canary: white wines.

headlands and islands of Boston Harbor came in sight.

While the Griffin passed the Brewsters guarding the narrow entrance to the harbor, toward which she had so long been holding her course, William and Anne gathered their young folks about them. Wooded islands appeared to them on the one hand and the other — Long Island, "Governor's Garden," Spectacle, Half-Moon, Castle, where they were building the new fort, Hog Island, and Noddle. There were islands aplenty, but the passengers of the Griffin had eyes mostly for the town at the mouth of the Charles, poor and mean and straggling though it must have looked to them.

To this town the Hutchinsons were bringing turmoil and division. However, the family that they were bringing with them looked like a useful addition to the life of a newborn colony. Edward, the eldest son, was already in Boston. With William and Anne came Richard, a youth of nineteen, and Faith, a maiden of marriageable age. Bridget and Francis, named for their Marbury grandparents, were sixteen and fourteen. Then came a parcel of younglings, beginning with Sam who was ten, and ending with Baby Susan; between these were Anne, Mary, Katherine and William. *If Anne Hutchinson had received a revelation of the tragic end that some of these boys and girls would share with her, her mother's heart would indeed have fainted at the thought of bringing them to a strange land.*

It was the 18th of September 1634, when the Griffin and her companion ship reached port in Boston. They had arrived with their two hundred settlers from Old Boston and vicinity and the one hundred cattle for John Winthrop. That day a stout, smiling, little man might have been seen stepping vigorously along a country road leading from his home down to the landing place at the foot of Fleet Street. His clothes proclaimed him a clergyman. His square, firm face with eyes far apart under a broad brow showed balance and fair-mindedness. The white hair did not make him an old man. John Cotton was forty-nine.

Cotton had preached that morning. The General Court had appointed the day to be one of humiliation and prayer. They were seeking God's guidance in solving the vexed problem as to whether they should allow Hooker and his Newtowne congregation to migrate to Connecticut. In his sermon, Mr. Cotton had clearly presented the case for both sides and then left it to the parties interested to make what application they desired. He was well content with the morning's work and was now looking forward, with pleasure, to welcoming some dear old friends of his to New England. The Griffin was coming to dock, bringing the two worthy preachers, Mr. Symmes and Mr. Lothrop, several friends and parishioners from Old Boston and the gifted and devout Mistress Anne Hutchinson of Alford. The Hutchinsons were "wheat fit for the planting of God's kingdom." Such a listener as Anne Hutchinson was an inspiration to any preacher — if she approved of him.

In 1634, the village of Boston was not so large but that each newcomer was a source of curiosity, congratulation, or caution on the part of those already established. It contained less than a thousand inhabitants. They lived in cabins and simple frame houses scattered among the hilly pastures of a little peninsula. Captain William Wood, a year later, described it as the chief place in New England for "shipments and merchandize."

"This necke of land," wrote Captain Wood, "is not above foure miles in compass, in form almost square, having at the south-side, at one corner, a great broad hill, whereon is planted a Fort, which can command any ship as she sayles into any Harbour within the still Bay. On the North-side is another Hill, equall in bignesse, whereon stands a Winde-mill. To the North-west is a high Mountaine with three little rising Hills on the top of it, wherefore it is called the Tramount. From the top of this Mountaine a man may overlooke all the Ilands which lie before the Bay, and descry such ships as are upon the

Seacoast.

"This towne, although it be neither the greatest nor the richest, yet it is the most noted and frequented, being the Center of the Plantations where monthly Courts are kept. Here likewise dwells the Governour: This place hath very good land, affording rich cornefields and fruitfull Gardens; having likewise sweete and pleasant Springs."

In spite of its "shipments and merchandize," its meetings of the General Court and the presence of the Governor, Boston was still, in 1634, a farming village.

In the fall of 1630, after a horrible summer of dysentery, death and disaster at Charlestown, Winthrop and the major portion of his company had chosen the peninsula for a town site. This decision was partly on account of William Blackstone's spring of sweet water and partly because it was so narrow that a very little fencing could secure their cattle from the wolves. "It being a necke and bare of woods, they were not troubled with three great annoyances, of wolves, Rattle-snakes and Musketoes."

In the summer, the Bostonians raised corn on their home lots. They kept their cows and pigs on their outlying farms in Muddy River, now Brookline, and other districts where they had meadows, marsh, and timber land. In the winter they brought their stock into town. The peninsula was not spacious enough for extensive farming but "fittest for such as can trade with England, for such commodities as the Countrey wants." Trade of this sort offered scope for the business experience of William Hutchinson, mercer.

The people of Boston tried to build a New England to look as much like Old England as possible. Their materials were scanty, and in 1634, there were only a few frame houses. William Coddington, Treasurer of the Colony, and a friend of Anne Hutchinson, owned the one home made of brick.

The greater part of the houses were still one room cottages of clay and logs. They were all built facing the south, with thatched roofs and the chimney at one end. When they were able, the settlers added another room, so that the chimney came in the middle. Under the roof was a loft. John Cotton, hurrying down to the landing, passed several such cottages. He caught glimpses of them scattered along the paths that led to the gristmill on Copp's Hill, to the common pasture on Sentry Hill, to the "spring-gate" in what is now called Spring Lane, and, above all, to the meeting house.

The irregularity of the paths troubled John Cotton's orderly soul and he found space in his crowded thoughts to note that Boston needed a town planning board. His wish was realized the next year in an ordinance, "That from this day there shall be noe house at all be built in this towne neere unto any of the streetes or laynes therein but with the advice and consent of the overseers — for the more comely and commodious ordering of them." The men who enforced the law must have been easily satisfied!

Mr. Cotton hastened along the dusty main road of the village toward the dock. His mind was full of the affairs of the colony. Besides the Reverend Mr. Hooker's yearning to withdraw to Connecticut with his Newtowne parishioners, there was a demand from England that the Massachusetts Bay Charter be yielded up — a demand that they must face. His active brain was considering and rejecting plan after plan for putting off the unlucky day when the beneficent charter would have to be relinquished. What to do if a Governor-General should arrive from England? What to do about Captain Underhill's laced sleeves and far from straight-laced morals? What to say when the women asked his advice on the subject of veils? About all these things, great and small, and many more, this busy and versatile gentleman was obliged to formulate a plan.

He reached the wharf in time, finding the two Edward Hutchinsons already there, watching the cautious approach of the vessel. Next to the sight of land after ten weeks or so in the crowded quarters of the Griffin — and next to the face of her firstborn — the most pleasant object that

Anne Hutchinson's eyes rested upon was the cheerful, rosy countenance of her beloved Mr. Cotton. They had removed her teacher into a corner, but now her eyes did indeed behold him again.

Edward shouted to his parents and brothers and sisters as they brought them ashore: William, Anne, their crowding and excited children, with two kinswomen named Anne and Francis Freiston and perhaps a servant or two that they had brought along. At last, the family group was complete. Parents and son embraced. Then the little throng paused in its bustle to watch the meeting between John Cotton and the woman who had already impressed her personality upon her fellow-passengers. After a year's separation, beloved teacher and loyal disciple were reunited. Pale from the limited fare and the confinement of the voyage, Anne was still full of eager words. She made no secret of the fact that she had come those three thousand watery miles for the sake of seeing Mr. Cotton and listening again to his sermons. Nor did he hide his gratification that this gifted, pious, wellborn lady, reared in a churchly and cultured atmosphere, had placed so high a value on his teaching.

The Hutchinsons found the Boston to which Mr. Cotton introduced them already a tiny metropolis to which a group of other communities looked. A dozen villages had sprung up in the valleys of the Charles and Mystic Rivers and along the seashore to the north and south. Some of them, like Salem, Dorchester, and Charlestown, were older than Boston, but Boston was the center of trade. All the villages together comprised four thousand inhabitants. They were still only a thin fringe, clinging to the edge of an unexplored wilderness. Nevertheless, they were fencing fields, roads were laid out, and bridges built. There was, after all, an English look about the little settlements.

North and south, the Atlantic seaboard had its edging of white men. South was Plymouth, with its few hamlets. In a palisaded fort on Noddle Island was Samuel Maverick, royal commissioner and Church of England man. Sixty miles to the north was Sir Ferdinando Gorges' colony at Saco, with six tiny fishing or trading stations and three hundred inhabitants. New Hampshire was more prosperous, made up of Rye, Dover and Portsmouth. Rhode Island was not yet. Connecticut was a couple of trading posts, a Dutch one at Hartford and a Plymouth offshoot at Windsor. That was New England.

New York was already a melting pot of Walloons* and Dutch, with Protestant religionists from all over Europe

* Walloons: one of a group of people inhabiting the southern and southeastern parts of Belgium and adjacent regions in France.

attracted by Dutch tolerance. At the mouth of the Potomac was the settlement of the Catholic aristocrat Calvert, a thorn in the flesh of Virginia. Virginia herself had weathered poor colonization and Indian attacks, and was already shipping enough tobacco to afford the King a convenient source of revenue.

In spite of its four thousand inhabitants, Massachusetts was still no place for the timorous and the ease-loving. Lynxes might sit on their doorsteps at night. Deer, raccoon, and even bears destroy their crops. Indians stalk, aloof but inquisitive, through their streets. Besides that, they had to deal with a climate such as they had never known before, either for heat or cold. A barber going from Boston to Roxbury to pull a man's tooth froze to death in his brief journey. Yet, summer brought days so hot that the people feared to go abroad except at night.

On the other hand, Francis Higginson, who was at Salem in 1629-30, wrote what sounds like modern real estate advertising in his *New England Plantation*. He wrote of the extraordinary dry and clear air of New England that healed many who were sickly in the old country. As for himself, he says that he now habitually went without a cap. He could formerly drink only strong, stale drink, now he could, and oftentimes did, drink New England water very well. He died the next year.

Like Anne Hutchinson, many New England Bostonians had come from Lincolnshire. Others came from adjacent counties. The settling of Massachusetts was altogether much of a family affair. Relatives and neighbors of the first comers were arriving every year. They were coming fast, too. Whole fleets of ships would reach Massachusetts Bay in a single month. Thus, one day in June of 1635, eleven ships arrived. News came from England at intervals of perhaps a week during good weather. The Hutchinsons were well known even when they landed and entered Boston society under the wing of John Cotton, who had no suspicion that they were going to cause him so much trouble.

William Hutchinson was promptly admitted to membership in the Boston church. In that theocratic community he could not have been a voter had he not been a church member. On May 18, 1631, it had been ordered by the General Court that "for time to come noe man shalbe admitted to the freedome of this body polliticke but such as are members of some of the churches within the limits of the same."

To the surprise of both William and Anne, they delayed her admission to the church, though only for one week, at the warning of Zachariah Symmes. On November 2, they inscribed her name, also, on the roll of the Boston church.

Anne and William went to live in the most select part of Boston. William's land was what has since been known as the Old Corner Book Store lot, at the northern corner of Washington and School Streets. In 1634, it was the corner of Market Street and a path leading to Sentry Hill. Back of the Hutchinsons' land toward "the highway to the Common," which is now Tremont Street, was the land of Mr. Thomas Scottow, where City Hall now stands. Further up Sentry Lane, which was not yet laid out, was the burying ground. Close by was Atherton Hough's house. A little to the northwest on Prison Lane, now Court Street, was the jail. Near by was the church on the south side of what is now State Street, with whipping post and stocks handy by. Almost across the road from the Hutchinsons' was Spring Lane with the great "Spring-Gate," a fenced-in water supply. On the south side of Spring Lane was Governor Winthrop's house.

Thus, being in the very heart of things gratified Anne's social instincts. At the spring, neighbors might congregate every few hours. Even living on the road to the burying ground and the jail had social advantages. Everybody in Boston must have passed her house frequently. Those from the outlying towns who came to Boston for business or pleasure went her way.

In January of 1636, and again in January of the next year, they made two grants of farm land to William Hutchinson, amounting in all to six hundred acres in Wollaston. They had retrieved the acreage from the grasp of the unpuritanical Morton and doled it out to good Bostonians. William Coddington, their friend and neighbor and later their comrade in the Rhode Island settlement, was one of the chief Wollaston grantees. He shared, with Edmund Quincy, the land fronting on Wollaston Bay. William Hutchinson also had a house and farm in Dorchester.

The house that William had built in Boston for his family on that fine corner lot faced the south as did most of the other houses. It looked as much like an English farmhouse as English carpenters and the building materials of a raw country could make it. In size, it was spacious enough to hold later the crowd of sixty or seventy who congregated at Anne Hutchinson's meetings. Perhaps William followed a custom of the time and had his place of business under the same roof with his residence. If so, the meetings that his wife instituted must have meant good trade for the shop. He had been promoted by this time from the rank of a mercer to that of a merchant.

Keen, energetic, competent, well-recommended, well-

known and well-to-do, Anne Hutchinson plunged into the life of this sturdy little community. The same that was building itself so snugly according to the will of the strong men who headed it. Anne was, unfortunately, a protester against their will and their way.

1. Three hundred years later, nothing had changed in the matter of shipping cattle overseas, in either direction.

Isadora Duncan (1878-1927) records in her autobiography *My Life* the trip from New York to England of herself and her family, about 1900. She wrote:

"It was Raymond [her brother] who had the bright idea of searching round the wharves until he found a small cattle boat going to Hull. . . . I believe that it was this trip which was the great influence in making Raymond a vegetarian, for the sight of a couple of hundred poor, struggling beasts in the hold, on their way to London from the plains of the Middle West, goring each other with their horns and moaning in the most piteous way, night and day, made a deep impression on us. . . . Only the bellowings and moanings of the poor cattle in the hold depressed us. I wonder if they still bring cattle over in that barbarous fashion."

VII

A SOCIAL LEADER

Inside of two years, Anne Hutchinson found herself at the center of everything that was happening in Boston. On the authority of John Winthrop, whom we can never accuse of flattering her, *she was the most popular woman in the colony, more resorted to "for counsell and advice than any of the ministers."*

The reasons for her popularity came both from within and from without. Among those of the latter sort was the fact that the right person introduced her into the society of the village capital. A newcomer sponsored by John Cotton and enjoying, not only his parochial courtesies, but his personal friendship, was sure to receive plenty of attention from those who considered themselves the best people in the town.

We must note, however, that there was always an important minority who did not come under Anne's spell. John Winthrop, father of the colony, even from the first, was not enthusiastic about her. Certainly he does not mention her in his history until he has something unfavorable to report. Perhaps he was too busy, too engrossed in many cares, to get enthusiastic about anyone, least of all about a woman. The Reverend John Wilson, pastor of the Boston church, also remained outside the circle of her influence. Perhaps he listened to Zachariah Symmes; perhaps her outspoken devotion to his associate Cotton hurt him. More likely the antagonism between Wilson and Anne Hutchinson was due to their temperaments, which were enough alike to make their differences more rasping. *They were both sure their way was right, but their ways diverged to the opposite poles. John Wilson's was conservative, legal, severe. Anne's was enthusiastic, mystical, something to be determined by the individual heart in private communion with God.*

Yet Wilson got on well with Cotton and had shown a generous spirit in accepting a colleague who came with a reputation that overshadowed his own. Within five weeks after Cotton's arrival in the colony, the Boston church had made him "teacher," fearing that they might lose him to another place if they were not prompt. The Puritans had been used to seeing two clergymen, a vicar or rector and a curate, in many churches at home. In the pastor-teacher plan the difference was that while the teacher expounded and the pastor looked after the flock, one was not subordinate to the other.

Cotton was slightly the senior in years and, because of his white hair and benign countenance, was the more reverend in appearance. Wilson, on the other hand, was the senior in term of service in Boston. He had been the pastor of the church even before it came to Boston, while it was still a wildwood congregation meeting under a tree in Charlestown. Since then he had served his charge continuously, except for the two trips that he made to England after his lady wife, the daughter of Sir John Mansfield, Master of the Minories. Cotton, on appointment, proved so tactful, so friendly and moderate, that he got on well with everyone, including Wilson. It was not long before they were consulting him on all kinds of questions and he became almost as influential in civil matters as in religious.

Besides deriving benefit from this friendship with Cotton, Anne Hutchinson found her social standing enhanced by her gentle birth.

In those years, Boston was far from being a democratic place. Democracy, either as a form of government or a social custom, was completely obnoxious to the founders. John Winthrop wrote, "The best part of a community is always the least; of that least part the wiser are still less." As for a democratic form of government, he denounced it as "the meanest and worst and so accounted among most civil nations." Accordingly, hard and meager as life was in the colony, where every man — and every woman, too

— had to lend a hand to actual labor, they never forgot social distinctions. Perhaps they meant all the more to men and women who no longer had ancestral homes or family plate to bear witness to their degree. For a long time, there was great sensitiveness about the use of the address "Mr." and only those whose birth or financial weight justified it received the appellation. Next below "Mr." came the "Goodman" and his "Goodwife." Below those, came the insignificant, almost anonymous "one" — "One Smith, a servant." Goodmen and the still humbler "ones" could have their inglorious feet put into stocks, their ears lopped off, their backs lacerated by the lash. Gentlemen who broke the law were merely fined.

Anne Hutchinson, daughter of the Marburys and granddaughter of the Drydens, had to give precedence, of course, to John Humphrey's wife, born Lady Susan Clinton, sister of the Earl of Lincoln. However, Lady Susan did not remain long enough to outrank the other colonial dames, for she disliked the New World. She early returned to England, leaving a young family to become a source of agitation to the town of Swampscott and the whole colony. The Earl's other sister, Arbella, wife of Isaac Johnson, had died at Salem, in that first summer of 1630, without ever getting as far as Boston. Anne Hutchinson had no need to give precedence to sweet

Margaret Winthrop, to Mary Coddington, Elizabeth Aspinwall, Elizabeth Hough, or to Anne Bradstreet, bluestocking daughter of Thomas Dudley.[1] In the account of her trial before the General Court four years later, she is punctiliously and repeatedly designated as "this gentlewoman."

She was not simply Anne Hutchinson, standing alone. She was the wife of William Hutchinson, deputy to the General Court from May 1635 to September 1636, and judge of the District Court. Yes, and a moneymaker. The Hutchinsons knew how to do that. Besides, she was the friend of the Coddingtons, the Houghs, and the Coggeshalls, and of the Cottons.

At the advice of such friends, the Hutchinsons settled in the fashionable quarter of Boston. It was near enough to the Cotton home so that the clergyman could often come and hold discourse with this brilliant and critical woman whose high regard could not help being flattering to any man. While they talked, William, the merchant, sat patiently by — "a man of weak parts and wholly influenced by his wife," Winthrop wrote slightingly. Still, William might have done worse. *Life with Anne must have been interesting.* It has been shrewdly observed that "men are led to believe whatsoever they believe by one of three things, their purses, their stomachs, or their wives."

115

William believed in Anne and he had the satisfaction of seeing far more brilliant men than he come under her guidance.

One of these was Harry Vane, son of the King's Privy Councilor. Young Vane came to Boston fourteen months after the Hutchinsons and, as a friend of John Cotton, became acquainted with Cotton's friends. His visit to America was due to the audacity with which he, hardly more than a boy, had faced Archbishop Laud. Refusing to take the oath of conformity necessary to matriculation at college, he had flung off to Geneva, the citadel of Calvin. Thence he had returned, so fortified with theological arguments that he dared dispute with Laud, he was threatened with the law, and in turn he threatened to migrate to Boston, "the Geneva on the Charles." His father consented, the Archbishop did not object, and the King granted him special permission to visit New England.

At this time Harry Vane was twenty-three, handsome, brilliant, an heir to a title, and unmarried. They describe him as having an oval face, with fair skin, a brow wide above a pair of dark eyes, lips full and red but faintly stern. His head was carried high and adorned with rich brown hair, which, alas, he had cut Puritan fashion after he came back from Geneva. How Boston maids and matrons must have fluttered! They had so little excitement of such a kind. Most of their thrills came from hardships. Indians and wolves might harass their imaginations, but rich, handsome, and aristocratic young men rarely came to their shores. Boston promptly did what it could for him in a social way and took him into the church. Within two months of his arrival, they voted that no one should sue another at law until Mr. Harry Vane and two elders should have heard the matter. The next year they made him governor. Because he was the son of a Privy Councilor, the ships in the harbor wasted a volley of their precious great shot in congratulation.

It was natural that Vane should pick out the best company that he could find in the frontier village. He made his home in the same house with John Cotton and he found congenial conversation in the society of Anne Hutchinson. *She was a lady, she was nimble of wit and subtle of mind, delighting as he did in finespun argument. What united them most closely was the fact that they were both "enthusiasts." They both believed that human beings of their own day could be inspired by God, that the Spirit dwelt in the Christian so that the two were one, and that truth was revealed to the Christian — at least, to some Christians — as it had been revealed to the prophets of old. To use the language of their day, they believed in "direct inspiration."[2] They were New England*

Transcendentalists, two hundred years ahead of their time.

Unfortunately for modern scandalmongers, there is no chance of making a purple patch* out of the friendship between Anne and the young governor. Vane was only a year older than her eldest son, she herself was forty-four and certainly no longer beautiful, if she had ever been. Nevertheless, they recorded, more than thirty years later, a strange and ugly attempt to connect scandal with the names of these two. Among the Colonial Papers of 1667, preserved in the British Public Record Office, in the handwriting of Sir Joseph Williamson, Under-Secretary and Secretary of State in the reign of Charles II, is this entry:

"Sir Harry Vane in 1637 went ov^r as Govern^r to N. Engl^d with 2 women, Mrs Duer and Mrs Hutchinson, wife to Hutchinson's brother, and he desbauched both, and both were delivered of monsters. Received ye K's Comiss^n then banished."

This is endorsed, "From Maj. Scott's mouth."

Well —! Anne Hutchinson came to America in September of 1634 and Harry Vane came in October 1635. Mary Dyer may have come on the same boat with Vane, but, even so, the statement of the Colonial Office entry

---

* Purple patch: a scandal.

is incorrect in at least two particulars. The "monsters," alas, have a little foundation in fact, though modern obstetrics would apply no such name to the unfortunate miscarriages that both these stainless matrons endured. However, the association of Vane's name with those events is a piece of political calumny written down in 1667, six years after the Stuart Restoration. It was five years after they had chopped off Harry Vane's gallant head because King Charles II thought him "too dangerous a man to let live, if we can honestly put him out of the way."

Besides John Cotton and Harry Vane and other wellborn and well-placed friends, Anne had a throng of humble admirers, bound to her by gratitude. She was Lady Bountiful, helpful in sickness and trouble to all the women she could reach, of whatever degree. She was skilled in nursing, trained to it by her duties in her father's home and in her own, by the needs of a city parish and of a country town. Besides being skillful, she was well-to-do, and besides being well-to-do, she was willing and tireless. Here was an outlet for her energy.

There was much sickness in the colony and, of course, babies were always being born. Anne soon acquired a reputation for wisdom in the hour of need, women's needs. Not only her syrups and tinctures, her broths and her cordials, but her buoyant words brought healing. To their homesick, aching hearts she was the teacher of a softer dispensation than that preached by their ministers or practiced by their husbands.

As Anne went about doing good, helping those who were sick or in trouble, it was natural that the women should open their minds to her and talk freely. There were so many vexations to talk about: sickness, Puritan husbands — or maybe just husbands — hordes of children, sumptuary laws* that took away their nicest clothes, the howling of wolves, the stinging of "musketoes," the lack of the kind of food to which they had been accustomed, the bitter winters, the oppressive summers, the vital question of wearing veils or not wearing them. The Reverend Roger Williams had preached that women should go veiled. The even more reverend John Cotton had preached them off again. What did Anne Hutchinson think about it?

Anne Hutchinson thought both Mr. Williams and Mr. Cotton were smiling up the sleeves of their Geneva gowns and preaching veils because the people were interested in them. No doubt she said so and the women laughed

---

* Sumptuary laws: designed to regulate habits, or luxurious clothing, on moral or religious grounds.

and realized their salvation, after all, did not depend upon veils.

Anne brought many topics out into the open. She gave the women a chance to express themselves. She herself never stopped talking. It is no wonder the women drew a new life from her vigorous strength, so generously expended. It helped too, that she was of gentle birth — helped tremendously.

In later years John Cotton, blamed for having been on her side, said, "At her first coming she was well respected and esteemed of me not only because herself and her family were well beloved in England at Alford in Lincolnshire; not only because herself with her family came over hither (as was said) for conscience sake: but chiefly that I heard she did much good in our Town, women's meetings, Childbirth-Travels, good discourse about their spiritual estates."

We must agree she had all these assets: good sponsors, breeding, money, kindness and skill in nursing. Nevertheless, all these would not have made her the kind of woman who becomes a leader paramount, one for whose principles sound men are willing to suffer banishment, had she not been able to secure personal allegiance. She was surely a woman of winning personality, of magnetism. With this natural gift added to her other resources, her social leadership was assured.

Nothing has ever been recorded about her appearance except that she was of a haughty carriage. References to her pride of bearing occur again and again, and since no one, friend or foe, missed a chance to mention it, we may conclude that it was a conspicuous characteristic. Had she been handsome, they would have handed down some hint of it as there was of Margaret Winthrop's sweetness, of Mary Dyer's beauty and winsome speech. But though Anne may have been plain of feature, she clearly had charm. She was the friend of the brilliant and dashing young Harry Vane; friend, though not always loyally defended, of the honey-sweet John Cotton; friend of Jane Hawkins, "notorious for her familiarity with the devil." She was a friend of the wise and the simple, the high and the low. Thomas Weld, who never intentionally said anything good of her, admitted that "she had some of all sorts and quality to defend and patronize." Ellis, her first biographer, says, "Nor, as far as can be discovered, did anyone become her enemy who was ever her friend." By the time she had been two years in her new home, she was drinking that most heady of all wines, the deference of her associates.

So her days in those first two years were happy as they were busy. She saw snowstorms such as she had never dreamed of in Lincolnshire; she experienced summer heat that almost quenched her. The constant dread of mysterious savages haunted her even in her times of greatest security. Try as hard as she might, she could not make her new home quite like Alford. The commonest comforts were either scarce or wholly unobtainable. Still, Boston was a little bit of England and her house was an English home.

Of a morning she rose early, put on her gown of strong black stuff and prayed in her cold room. Then she saw that her children were roused from their trundle beds and pallets and got into their plain, stiff clothes. Breakfast was a negligible affair, as it was in England at that time. The family did not sit at table but everybody had a bit of bread. The elders had wine, or more likely, ale; the youngsters, eating docilely after their parents, had milk, frequently clabbered. William led his family in prayer.

Then Anne saw that the family became busy. There were so many things to be done — the preparation of food, looking after the supplies of corn from the Wollaston farm, making and mending of clothes for the small army that her house contained, candle-moulding, curing of meats, preparation of cordials and medicines. Although there were many hands to do the work, the head was Anne's. She had to train what servants she was able to get; she had to instruct her children. The younger ones went off in the dusk of early morning to a dame school, but at home they had to be taught to knit and spin and make candlewicks.

In the midst of a busy morning, news would come that some neighbor's baby was on the way. Could Anne Hutchinson come at once?

So Anne would set out. She might find wheedling Jane Hawkins already on hand to give her midwifely aid. Still, the mother would want spiritual comfort as well as physical attention. Anne could not stay through all the long agony. Nevertheless, she could straighten out the disordered household, let the tortured wife cling to her for a while, and hurry home to her noonday meal with her family. Then she would get back to the house of birth again in time to slap the newborn babe and set him into a suitable and supposedly healthful wail of protest.

Yet this was not all of a day's work. A poor young woman down the road was sick with consumption and afraid to die and leave her little children to the stepmother that the goodman would get with conscientious haste. The sick woman would need mothering. She would need someone to say confidently to her, "God is Love and you are His dear child." She would need someone to say, "Your children will not forget you and you will surely see them all in Heaven." This Anne could do with conviction, unmindful of what the ministers might say about God's elect, about preordaining some to salvation and others to damnation. Anne could gather the poor girl into her arms and pour into her the strength of her confident and highly charged personality. Perhaps the sick one wanted to make a confession, to acknowledge that she had loved pretty clothes, had loved to dance, had surely been of a light and wayward spirit.

"Dear child, do not grieve," Anne would say. "Do you love our Lord?" The sufferer would nod her head against the mothering shoulder. "Then His Spirit is in you. The love that is in your heart is true religion. Do you not remember His Word, that the fruit of the Spirit is Love [Galatians 5:22]? Love is of God, and everyone that loveth is born of God. Be not afraid, my child." So she preached her gentle doctrine of love and sanctification by faith to her sisters in the colony.

From such ministrations as these she would return to meet John Cotton and Governor Vane at her door. She was full of the blessed experience that she had had and must tell of it. They would go in and listen — Cotton cautiously, dubiously smiling, Vane warmhearted and enthusiastic, quick to follow the windings of her mysticism. Young as he was, Vane was versed in such subtleties. He, too, believed that God sometimes spoke directly to his true followers, not by outward signs and portents, but directly to the loving heart. It was more than direction and inspiration, it was identity, oneness with the Spirit, that made this possible. "Hereby know we that we dwell in Him and He in us, because He hath given us of His Spirit," Vane would quote from the First Epistle of John 4:13. "Whosoever shall confess that Jesus is the Son of God, God dwelleth in him, and he in God." (1 John 4:15.) Anne could match Scripture for Scripture. "I and my Beloved are one." (John 10:30.) But Cotton, still gently smiling, would shake his head and try to bring the two down to earth. He could quote Scripture longer than anyone else. "If you love me, keep my commandments." (John 14:15.) And again, "By their fruits ye shall know them." (Matthew 7:20.)

"The fruits of your labors are rich and plentiful," the young Governor would say as he rose. He bowed profoundly to his hostess and only a little less so to his reverend friend and went off to pay some more official, and more irksome, call.

Cotton lingered, for he had a duty to perform. It was his task to deliver a rebuke — at least a piece of advice — to this paragon of his flock. Since it had to be done, let it be done at once, but privately. A matter had been brought to his attention which he must pass on, reluctant as he was, to this brilliant and devout woman of his congregation. Was Anne Hutchinson aware that there had been a prayer meeting last evening at a house near by?

Yes, she did know of it.

Then did she know that they had noted her absence? Some had wondered that Anne Hutchinson should hold herself aloof from such an instrument of grace. "Surely it could not have been for pride, dear friend?" (It was part of Cotton's duty to probe the hearts of his people.) "Not pride of this world, dear lady — though some did hint at that — but perhaps — pride of the spirit is no less hateful to our Lord than pride of place. Despise not the gathering together of two or three in His name. Nay, I know well that you do not, sister. It is only that those who would use their gifts to the full glory of God must shun even an appearance of evil."

With this benediction Mr. Cotton departed, satisfied that he had done his duty. Anne had flushed and controlled her tongue with difficulty. Reproof, even from her beloved teacher, sat ill upon her spirit. Pride waved its banner unmistakably in the measured tones and the formality of her farewell.

While she went about her evening tasks, her quick resentment died down, but the rebuke lingered. When everything was quiet, the supper eaten, the children put away, the last call upon her time appeased, she followed her usual custom of sitting down to examine her conscience. She found it clear upon one point, that pride never kept her away from humble homes when they needed her. Yet, conscience rankled. Was it true that she would visit the lowly when she could help them, could confer favors, but not when her presence might have a social aspect? To tell the truth, she had not thought of going to the meeting. It offered slight inspiration to the women who attended. Men, and men only would speak, would recount their experience, would offer prayer. *The women, obeying the ordinance of Saint Paul, would keep silence as they did everywhere else, except at home.*

Anne meditated on the meagerness of social intercourse and sources of inspiration for the women of her village. As she sought to prove that a spirit of pride had not kept her aloof, her active mind discovered a way of solving the two problems at the same time. Why not hold meetings in her own house and hold them particularly for women?

As she dwelt upon the idea, she thought better and better of it. It would give the women something of their very own. They could have it to cherish and look forward to, they could at last freely express themselves. Mr. Cotton could not accuse her of pride, for she would invite all who wished to come, from Margaret Winthrop down to Jane Hawkins. No one should be left out, though she was most concerned for those whom family cares kept from attending the church services.

Perhaps John Cotton, if he had been at hand, might have pointed out the social distinction between inviting the women to her home and going to theirs. It was one thing to throw her doors magnificently wide to all who could be helped by enjoying her hospitality, and another thing to put on her bonnet and cape and sit mutely with a homely little company of men and women in some other house. Or perhaps Cotton would merely have said that her generous impulse to ask the women of the village to attend meetings in her house was exactly what he would have expected of her, in perfect accord with her position, her circumstances, and her gifts. Nevertheless, in later years, he did not scruple to refer to her pride.

1. Anne Bradstreet was the first poet to appear in America, in the Massachusetts Bay Colony. Her volume *The Tenth Muse Lately Sprung Up in America* was the first volume of original verse to be written in America. It shows a sensitivity to beauty not usually associated with the Puritans.

2. The word *enthusiasm* comes from the Greek *enthousiasmos*, from *enthousiazein*, to be inspired, from en *(in)* + theos *(god/God)*. First

used in the year 1603 in English. The first definition given in *Webster's Ninth New Collegiate Dictionary* is: "belief in special revelations of the Holy Spirit."

VIII

FIRST WOMEN'S CLUB IN AMERICA

N eighborhood criticism, delivered ever so gently through the mouth of John Cotton, thus became the source of a startling innovation. It led Anne Hutchinson to found what we may fairly call the first women's club in America.

The situation of the women of the village was a subject of intense anxiety to her. As soon as she arrived, she began to do what she could for their bodily comfort and safety. She saw the high rate of female mortality. She heard that of the Plymouth settlers only four of the original eighteen wives were living at the end of the first year. Plymouth conditions were harder than those in the Bay Colony, but wellborn or humble, the wives of the pioneers everywhere were short-lived. Too many children, too much hard work, too little recreation, homesickness, monotonous diet,[1] these were more obvious hardships. Even the rigor of an icy meeting house endured for several hours, twice a week was no laughing matter. Besides these, there were difficulties inherent in the nature of the philosophy under which they lived. The flippant epigram — our New England foremothers had to endure, not only what our forefathers endured, but our forefathers as well — has some justification in fact. New England men had little time to waste on the graces and small courtesies of life. They did not recognize the restorative value of play. Play was of the devil. Nevertheless, the men who shared this hard existence with their wives did at least have more fresh air and warmer clothing. And they did not have to bring babies into the world biennially, perhaps annually.

Anne went out among the sick because her sympathy and her active temperament drove her to it. It was not a pleasant job. Nursing in those ill-heated, poorly ventilated, and sparsely equipped houses was no matter for daintiness. It required hand-to-hand grappling with all the unsavory details of personal service under the most inconvenient and distasteful circumstances.

Often in Winthrop's *History of New England* we run across the record: "The wife of ——, a godly woman, became distracted."[2] Winthrop was using the word distracted literally. He really meant that they were so torn asunder in their minds that they did not know what they were doing. Some of them, in time, became insane and in their madness took to violence. In 1637, Hett's wife, "distracted," took her babe and threw it into a well. The next year, Dorothy Talbye, "falling into a melancholy," slew her little daughter; more than one woman sought self-destruction. For these deeds, if they lived, they were made to suffer the utmost penalty of the law. Anne probably did not apprehend the full extremity into which these women might fall, but she was very early dissatisfied with the state of her sisters in the colony. *With her, to see that something was wrong meant an immediate effort to change it. She never shirked responsibility.* So she set to work to discover some way of providing recreation and stimulus for the women. Since they had criticized her for not attending the neighborhood prayer meeting, it happened that she could accomplish two ends with one means. She would clear herself of the charge of exclusiveness and encourage the women at the same time, by holding meetings for them in her own house.

So, Anne sent word about the village and the women responded gladly enough.

The meetings were, at first, especially intended for women who were unable to get to church. In every home there was almost always someone who was sick, or being born, or too tiny to be left alone. Therefore, many women were deprived of the sole recreational and cultural facility available in the town. The main diversions of Boston were two — going to church on Sunday and going to church on Thursday. For those who had the time and means for travel, it was also possible to go about to weekly lectures in other towns. In this way some of the colonists were able to pick up considerable entertainment. They were as indefatigable about it as a veteran bridge player of the present day who makes the round of all the charity card parties of the season. Going to meeting was a social event. After the sermon it was the custom to allow questions and discussion, but only male members participated in this pastime. Women were definitely understood to be in a "state of subjection." There were the private prayer meetings, but here too, the sisters had to keep silent. Marriages were civil ceremonies. The relatives conducted funerals, without benefit of clergy and with scant ceremony. Women might share in the public excitement of an ordination or the founding of a new church, but such occasions were naturally rare. There was almost no opportunity for them to express their social instinct.

Possibly, we have overestimated the fervent interest that the early Puritans took in their souls. Like the rest of the world, they were busy getting food and shelter, marrying and having children and seeing that their children got as large a slice of worldly possessions as possible. More than half the enactments at the Roxbury town meeting during the first four or five years were concerned with the fencing off of their respective lots of land. They worshiped God, but they were much occupied in keeping their earthly property free from trespass. They were not interested in the fine arts, or in pleasure as an art. Even literature found New England a milkless nurse. It remained for religion to be the New Englander's art and his pleasure.

This assertion can be made comprehensively, too, in the face of such a special instance as Captain John Underhill, a member of the Boston church, a Hutchinson man, and an unregenerate. The hardened old sinner told the church committee, who accused him of locking himself into the house with the cooper's pretty wife, that he was praying with her. "Queer the door was locked!" remarked his fellow members, who were not babes and sucklings.

If one considers the crimes, capital and other, listed in the Massachusetts Civil Code drawn up in 1651 by the Reverend Nathaniel Ward of Ipswich, it seems as if the saintly compiler must have possessed a ripe knowledge of both the world and the underworld. Nowhere could he find refuge from the wickedness that burneth as a fire except in religion, a refuge limited by Calvinistic doctrine to the least part of humankind. Yet for everybody in Massachusetts, the elect and the non-elect alike, religion had to replace books, theaters, and social gatherings.

It is surprising that the Puritans kept their feet on the

ground as well as they did. The reason is that their heads were hard and the chief men in particular had a good stock of natural balance and solidity. They were, in the main, a sagacious lot. They might err on the side of severity, but not on the side of enthusiasm or flightiness. A general moderation in all things characterized Winthrop and Cotton, the two most persistently influential men. In fact, the great reason for the clash between Anne Hutchinson and Winthrop was his conviction that she did not keep her feet upon the ground. He was afraid that the colony would be tempted into vagaries and exuberances, all of which he viewed with the distaste of a solid man. Anne's nature was bigger — and under less perfect control.

Her ready tongue ached with the restraint put upon it. She became convinced that an injustice was being done, that lack of self-expression was dwarfing the souls of the sisters. Here was a chance for them, for her, for all of them. To her house on a Monday she invited them, to come and talk over the sermon of the preceding Sunday. The first potential women's club in America was a Monday club. Later it became so popular that it met twice a week, on Mondays and Thursdays. It was a brilliant idea and a brilliant success.

They thronged her meetings. Here was something new, a break in the routine of the week, a chance to see one another. Of course the women all went. They were thrilled. It was the first real recreation that they had had since they left their native land — and no one knew for how much longer.

In a little while, however, the meetings ceased to belong exclusively to the women. They were too good to be missed and men began to attend. Charming Mr. Vane, the youthful governor, lent the sunshine of his presence, and we may suppose that the women enjoyed their meetings even more. At first, the clergy declared the gatherings to be a gift of heaven. They foresaw a glorious religious revival. Even Pastor Wilson was pleased and he congratulated Teacher Cotton upon being responsible for so dear an instrument of grace as Mrs. Hutchinson. "She was well beloved," wrote Cotton, "and all the faithful embraced her conference and blessed God for her fruitful discourse." Mr. Vane and Mr. Cotton, Mr. Dummer and Mr. Coddington, the deputies who came to General Court from other towns, Captain Underhill forsaking his pleasures for the time, these and many more of the foremost men of the colony were among those present. In the words of the Reverend Thomas Weld, who was emphatically not one of her court, "She had some of all sorts and quality in all places to defend and patronize her opinions, some of the magistrates, some gentlemen, some scholars and men of learning, some burgesses of our General Court, some of our captains and soldiers, and some men eminent for religion, parts and wit."

Wherever Governor Vane went, Boston society would not be far behind.

This was the particular moment in Anne's life celebrated by John Winthrop when he said that more resorted to her for counsel and advice about matters of conscience than to any minister in the colony. She herself declared that she could tell by half an hour's talk with a man whether he was "elected" or not.

"Come along with me," wrote Edward Johnson in his *Wonder-Working Providence* — satirizing, not inaccurately, the feelings if not the very words of her admirers — "and I'll bring you to a woman that preaches better Gospell than any of your black-coats that have been at the Ninnyversity, a woman of another kind of spirit, who hath had many revelations of things to come, and for my part, I had rather hear such a one that speaks from the meere motion of the spirit, without any study at all, than any of your learned Scollers, although they may be fuller of the Scripture."

The fact is, it would have been hard to find anyone fuller of the Scripture than Anne!

Sitting in her great chair, Anne repeated the sermon

that she had heard at the last church service. They conveniently wrote the sermons of those days with headings and subheadings. It was the custom to take notebooks to church. They expected even the children to repeat the morning sermon as part of their Sunday afternoon tasks. Anne was blessed with an unusually good memory and skill at reporting. The other women were delighted and thrilled at hearing a woman "exercise." Doubtless many were shocked, but agreeably so; it was something new. At first Anne's summary constituted the entire program of her women's club. Then someone ventured to ask a question and she answered. She explained what the preacher said. She added a little paraphrase of her own, then a little amendment. From that, it was a short step to expressing her independent opinion and, after that, inevitably came criticism of the preacher's words. It was perfectly natural and purely involuntary. What else could have been expected with Anne's ready tongue and wit and her long acquaintance with religious forensics?

"What she repeated (of the sermons) and confirmed was accounted sound; what she omitted was accounted Apocrypha." Thus, Cotton reported. From Thomas Weld comes another fuller and livelier description:

"Last and worst of all of the heresies of the colony which most suddainly diffused the venom of their opinions into the very veins and vitals of the people in the Country, was Mistress Hutchinson's double-weekly lecture, which she kept under a pretence of repeating sermons, to which resorted sundry of Boston and other Townes about, to the number of fifty, sixty or eighty at once; whereafter she had repeated the Sermon, she would make her comment upon it, vent her mischievous opinions as she pleased, and wreathed the Scripture to her owne purpose; where the custome was for the Scholars to propound questions, and she (gravely sitting in the chair) did make answer thereunto."

The picture, sharpened by animosity, is clear enough!

"Hence many families were neglected and much time lost." This is John Winthrop's contribution to the subject. He did not like intellectual women. Too much attention to reading and writing, too little to household affairs and such things as belong to women, he considered likely to unseat the reason of a female. His criticism that women's clubs occasion the neglect of families is not even yet wholly extinct.

News of Anne's meetings spread throughout the colony and those who could find means of attending came from other towns. Anne was a happy woman, sought after, delightfully busy, an inventor, a creator who had put new life into her small world. She was now on the very crest of the wave.

There she rode when in May 1636, a kindred spirit arrived from England, her brother-in-law, the Reverend John Wheelwright.

1. Not only a monotonous diet, but one deficient in essential nutrients. Today in the U.S., we have fresh fruits and vegetables all year around. That was an unthinkable dream then.

2. Why should these early New England wives and mothers become "distracted" or insane? A deficient diet, a harsh climate, a harsh religion, harsh husbands, with no respite from childbearing. Babies were born every seventeen months to two years — so many little ones to nurse, feed, clothe, care for. These large broods of children, this life without recreation or pleasure of any kind, brought some to insanity, even murder of their offspring, or suicide. This, Anne Hutchinson saw. This, her heart moved her to alleviate as much as she could, with compassioinate works, and a God-sent inspiration in religious thought she shared with the women of the Colony.

IX

THE FIRST SETBACK

Anne's meetings were the social events of the colony, as well as its intellectual stimulant. Her house was too small for all who wanted to get in and the overflow listened at the windows and doors. She continued opening the meeting with a summary of the previous Sunday's sermon. However, each week the vigor and range of her criticisms increased. She had a plan for improving the ministrations of the Boston church. A wonderful opportunity had arisen to secure exactly the right teacher for it — not to supplant the beloved John Cotton, but to assist him, and to neutralize the effect of Wilson's sermons, which she liked less and less.

This opportunity was the arrival in Boston of John Wheelwright.

Through his marriage to Mary Hutchinson, sister of William, Wheelwright was Anne's brother-in-law. He was a Cambridge graduate and college-mate of Oliver Cromwell, who is reported to have said of him, "I remember the time when I was more afraid of meeting Wheelwright at football, than I have been since of meeting an army in the field, for I was infallibly sure of being tripped by him." Cotton Mather also mentions Wheelwright's more than ordinary "stroke at wrestling" when he was in college.

This fighting youth grew to be a fighting parson. Before the Hutchinsons left England, he came under suspicion of being a nonconformist. One of Anne's minor reasons for pulling up stakes was the fact that her brother Wheelwright had been removed from his parish at Bilsby, close by Alford. For nearly three years he went about preaching secretly, with no fixed abode, until in the early summer of 1636 he made up his mind to go to America. On May 26, he arrived in Boston with his wife and family, and with Grandma Hutchinson, whose husband had died five years before.

When Anne received word that the Wheelwrights were coming, she was delighted and began to prepare the way for their cordial welcome. She early broached her project for the spiritual advancement of Boston and the worldly advancement of her brother-in-law to her friend, the governor. "Here is a minister," she said, "who thinks as you and I do. He, too, believes that the Holy Ghost actually dwells in the heart of every true Christian."

Governor Vane was what was known to the theologians of his time as a "seeker." That is, he was one not contented with any sect or creed but continually seeking a new one. Naturally a mystic, he heartily embraced Anne Hutchinson's opinions, went as far as she did, and a little further. Besides believing in an actual union between the Holy Ghost and the Christian, they both held that a good life, no matter how scrupulous its performance, did not prove a man to be a Christian. As they expressed it, "sanctification is no evidence of justification." The real evidence, they believed, was the personal consciousness of God's presence in the heart. Since nobody can tell about that except the individual concerned, there was no way by which outsiders could determine whether or not a man was a Christian. That *was* upsetting.

The older historians are handy with such terms as sanctification and justification. They take it for granted that their readers know what they mean. Less instructed twentieth century readers need to be informed that a justified person meant one chosen by God to be saved; that is, one of God's elect, one whom He had covenanted to save out of the general damnation entailed by Adam's fall. The Calvinistic doctrine taught that not all the sons of men should be saved but only such as the Creator "elected" to spare. It has been wickedly but effectively summarized in the doggerel:

"We hope too many won't be saved —

A number must be damned;
We'd better send some more below,
We can't have Heaven crammed."

It is about this time that the first actual mention of Anne Hutchinson's name occurs, except in church records. It is an entry in Winthrop's *History of New England*, dated October 21, 1636:

"One Mrs. Hutchinson, a member of the church of Boston, a woman of ready wit and bold spirit, brought over with her two dangerous errors: 1. that the person of the Holy Ghost dwells in a justified person. 2. that no sanctification can help to evidence to us our justification. From these two grew many branches; as (1) our union with the Holy Ghost, so as a Christian remains dead to every spiritual action, and hath no gifts nor graces, other than such as are in hypocrites, nor any other sanctification but the Holy Ghost himself. There joined with her in these opinions a brother of hers, one Mr. Wheelwright, a silenced minister sometime in England."

This sounds condemnatory but nebulous. To John Winthrop it meant something, at least enough to be put into words. To Anne Hutchinson also it meant something — something she had to defend at the cost of personal liberty. To almost everyone in the colony it meant something different.

Vane — young, ardent, sensitive, responsive to spiritual influences — needed only a suggestion to see that the addition of Wheelwright to the preaching force of the Boston church was just what they needed. To the ministrations of John Wilson, pastor, and John Cotton, teacher, Anne proposed to add the services of John Wheelwright, to assist Cotton in expounding the Scripture at the many meetings so eagerly desired by the people. Vane assured her that he would help to the extent of his ability.

Anne talked up her plan among her wide body of friends. On a Sunday late in October, at the church meeting which directly followed the service, they made the project public. According to custom a week was allowed for thinking it over. Sometime during that period, the ministers of the colony privately questioned Wheelwright as to his stand on the two doubtful points that were agitating them all: the indwelling of the Holy Ghost and sanctification. His answers did not satisfy them. He took a middle stand, not quite agreeing with his inquisitors on the one hand, or with Anne Hutchinson and Governor Vane on the other. It was, in fact, very nearly the ground that Cotton held, but the distinctions, too fine to be understood, were not too fine to be considered important. Whatever John Cotton may have thought about this attempt of his friend Anne Hutchinson to supply him with a colleague, he said nothing against it. Wilson, however, violently opposed it.

The next Sunday, Anne went to church hopeful that her project would succeed. She heard the motion made for accepting Wheelwright's appointment. Then she saw John Winthrop rise to speak and her heart sank. Winthrop spoke moderately and with courtesy, but his meaning was clear enough. He said that they were already well supplied with ministers, and that, anyway, they ought not to take one of whose opinions they were not sure. He had hardly sat down when Governor Vane sprang to his feet in the pew where he was accustomed to sitting in state with an escort of halberdiers.* Anne turned her encouraging face toward him.

"I am surprised that you speak thus," cried Vane, "when Mr. Cotton has already approved of these opinions." Anne looked hopefully at her friend Cotton, but Cotton refused to be drawn into it. He said he did not remember

---

* Halberdiers: soldiers carrying halberds — weapons, especially of the 15th and 16th centuries, consisting typically of a battle-ax and pike mounted on a handle about six feet long.

exactly what he had said on the subject, but wouldn't Mr. Wheelwright explain his opinions.

The congregation pricked up its ears, liking a debate, but sympathizing almost to an individual with Anne Hutchinson's candidate. Winthrop perceived this air of pleased expectancy and dampened it before Wheelwright could speak. Winthrop said that they ought not to take a teacher who was likely to be a cause of dispute. This was a blow, because a dispute was exactly what they enjoyed.

"Would it not be better," Winthrop suggested mildly, "to reserve Mr. Wheelwright for the new church which we are going to establish in Wollaston? We have a petition for a chapel of ease for the accommodation of worshipers in that quarter and God in His wisdom has sent our brother Wheelwright in His own just time."

This seemed a way of saving everybody's face. Most of the members were of Anne's opinion. Nevertheless, they were still a little shy of going in direct opposition to Winthrop, who, after all, was the Father of the colony. In fact the Wollaston landowners, some of whom were chief among the Wheelwright-Hutchinson party, such as Coddington, Hough, even William Hutchinson, may have had in mind a possible rebuff and had their petition for the Wollaston chapel ready. At any rate, the Boston church accepted Winthrop's suggestion and gave Wheelwright up to the new church. At that meeting they recorded that "our brother, Mr. John Wheelwright, was granted unto the preparing of a church gathering at Mount Woolystone, upon a petition from some of them that were resident there."

They carried out the arrangement and the Wollaston congregation welcomed Wheelwright.

Anne and her Boston friends, acquiescing but offended, ventured to take out some of their vexation in open criticism of Winthrop. The result of their talking was that he stood in meeting the next Sunday and begged them not to use "words and phrases of human invention," expressions such as "union with Christ" and "the person of the Holy Ghost," which he did not find in the Bible. "Let us not talk about this in church anymore," he urged. "But I shall be glad to talk it over in private with any brother who needs light."

To put it plainly, he asked for the last word in public.

Meanwhile, the rejection of Wheelwright became the chief topic of discussion at Anne's meetings. These were now more popular than ever. They fed on controversy and the meetings fed the controversy. Anne found herself definitely at the head of a faction. The whole town, even those who knew nothing about it, talked only of union with the Holy Ghost and sanctification.

A serious condition had arisen, portentous for an infant colony. Boston was divided into two camps. One rallied around Anne and her brother-in-law and numbered among its star supporters stout Captain Underhill, who was less credit spiritually than temporally; John Cotton — for the time; and Governor Vane. With these were ranged all but five of the members of the Boston church. On the other hand, the numbers of the opposition were small but mighty under the leadership of Pastor Wilson and the inexorable Thomas Dudley. To this party John Winthrop positively belonged, but in respect to Cotton he tried to act as intermediary. He was, above all, anxious to end a dispute that seemed to him trivial. It was hard enough to look after the colony, keep it alive and prevent interference from the mother country, without having to take issue on fine-spun theories. He forgot that in a state built on Biblical law there were sure to be varying interpretations of that law.

If John Winthrop was troubled, so was Anne. She not only had the matter of Wheelwright to hurt her pride, but she was concerned now for the credit of her young friend, Governor Vane.

Dissension had arisen in the Governor's Council. The members did not like him as well as they had at first. He made more show, assumed more state than their former governors, Winthrop, Dudley, and Haynes, who had been plain men like themselves. The respect and applause that they had given him at first were slackening, and Vane was beginning to realize it. He offered a kind of tentative resignation. There was a perfunctory demur. Vane wept and said he would never have thought to going had he not feared that the colony would hold him responsible for the disputes that had arisen. He said he dreaded God's judgement upon them for their quarrels and that, after all, business was really calling him home. Upon hearing his response, the Court voted to accept his resignation and call a special meeting to elect his successor.

Here Anne and her friend took a hand. As whole-heartedly as she had given up England if John Cotton could not be there, she now declared that New England would be unendurable if Mr. Vane should go. Some influential members of the church held a meeting and petitioned their young governor not to leave. He reconsidered and said that without the consent of the church he could not go. In fact, the majority of the Court and the colony probably wanted Vane to stay. The special meeting called to elect his successor was not held and he served out his term until the usual spring elections.

Meanwhile, the meetings at Anne Hutchinson's house went on, becoming ever more popular. Liking Mr. Wilson less and less, Anne can hardly be expected not to have used her dangerous wit in her summaries of his sermons. The crowd, packed into her rooms, appreciated her sallies, but it was not merely entertainment that they sought and found. *Anne taught a religion of love, as contrasted with the established doctrine of law and judgment. She placed reliance on an inner serenity and assurance of God's goodness. "If you have the Grace of God in your souls, you cannot displease Him. Get your heart right, and you cannot sin." No wonder her teaching was welcome! It brought joy and peace that the Puritans had not found in all their conning of the Bible, their rigid rules, their mint, anise, and cummin,* and it won many followers.*

By October of 1636, Winthrop wrote: "All the congregation of Boston, except four or five, closed with these opinions, or most of them; but one of the brethren (this was Winthrop himself) wrote against them, and bore witness to the truth, together with the pastor, and very few others joined with them."

---

* Matthew 23:23 (New King James Version) "Woe to you, scribes and Pharisees, hypocrites! For you pay tithe of mint and anise and cummin, and have neglected the weightier matters of the law: justice and mercy and faith. These you ought to have done, without leaving the others undone."

So Anne stood at the height of her power. With the Governor, Mr. Cotton and almost the whole church on her side, she had arrayed against her only a minister (to be sure, he was the pastor of the Boston church) and a deputy-governor (to be sure, he was Winthrop, father of the colony) and "very few others." *She urged her friends not to trust to gifts and graces, which are only a "legal way"; she taught them to seek the witness of the Spirit, to trust a Covenant of Grace, placed in their hearts by Christ, who departing said to his followers (John 16:7), "My comforter I leave with you." Mother of New England Transcendentalism, she said in effect, "Get your mental attitude right and your conduct will be right."*

The subtleties of the discussion tore the whole town. Everyone who professed to have any intellect at all improved upon the original contention by adding his contribution to the tangle and sounding abroad his own special opinion.

Ellis says, "The watchwords of the new party were heard everywhere, at town meetings, trainings, in public worship, in the blessing before meat, and the grace after meat." Children asked each other whether their parents stood for "grace" or "works," as they now ask whether they are Republican or Democrat.

"So the faithful ministers of Christ," wrote Thomas

Weld, "must have dung cast in their faces, and be no better than legal preachers, Baal's priests, Popish factors, scribes, Pharisees, and opposers of Christ himself."

Opposition brought out the combative strain in Anne. Indignant at the rejection of her Wheelwright proposition, and daily growing more sensitive about preaching that she disliked, she let her too ready tongue run away with her. She declared that there were only two ministers in the whole colony who were sealed with the covenant of grace.

These two, of course, were her friend Cotton and her brother Wheelwright. The rest, poor men, were laboring under a covenant of works. She could not abide their preaching, and when Wilson with his heavy utterance rose in the pulpit to give his sermon, she walked out of the church. So did others. We cannot expect that they made their departure inconspicuous.

The faithful ministers of the colony, thus having dung cast in their faces, were also indignant. In self-defense they were driven to find some ill name for Anne Hutchinson's beliefs. Readily, there came to their minds a scare-word of the time, Antinomianism. In all ages, when rebels have once been labeled, they seem even more terrifying to the conservative. So Anne and her associates, having been stamped Antinomians, became automatically something to be viewed with alarm, a menace, a "peril."

X

ANTINOMIANISM!

History has named the turmoil that seethed around Anne Hutchinson "The Antinomian Controversy." We cannot escape the use of that appalling word nor some explanation of it.

It was a terrible thing to be called an Antinomian. The feeling in the mind of one who hurled that epithet in 1636 was like that of one who yelled "Bolshevik" or "Red" in the 1930's in the United States. The Antinomians were the bogies of the Puritan fathers. They were regarded as the enemies not only of the church but of the state.

If one goes back to the Latin derivation of the word, Antinomian means an opposition to literalism, from *anti*, against, and *nomen*, name. In the church of Anne Hutchinson's time it meant rejecting the literal "Law" of the Old Testament for the spiritual "Gospel" of the New. That, of course, is what all Christians do in theory. It was what the New England Puritans professed to have done, but they, following Calvin, had built up their theocratic system on the Mosaic Law of the Old Testament. That was their working plan and Antinomianism interfered with it.

A literal or even an ecclesiastical interpretation of the word was not enough to strike such terror. Its connotations made the fathers of the colony gird on their fighting gear. By reputation Antinomianism included a great deal more than a mere substitution of the Grace of the New Testament for the Law of the Old. It represented a whole brood of strange opinions, all the hydra-headed sects that had issued in the last hundred years from Central Europe, had spread to England and taken refuge in Holland. Antinomians, Anabaptists, Familists, Adamites, Libertines, Opinionists, they were all tarred with the same brush. They were all lumped together under the one, long, hard, indiscriminate name in the minds of the leaders of the New England colony. *The gentle words of Anne Hutchinson, that holiness was a matter of the heart,* called to the memory of ministers and the elders the incendiary teachings of Knipperdoling and John of Leyden.

It seems absurd that an affair that happened a hundred years before in Munster of Westphalia* could have left such a terrifying tradition. The Munster affair, in which John of Leyden played the star role, was, briefly, an attempt by the Anabaptists (anti-militarists and gentle, humble communists who called each other brother and held all

---

* Westphalia: a former Prussian province of western Germany.

things in common) to set up a government of their own in Munster. Having obtained control of the city council, abolished cathedral and convents and driven out all but Anabaptists, they attracted to themselves adherents of half a hundred other creeds. Of course they fell into dissension and were ripe fruit for some demagogue to pluck. The demagogue appeared in the person of John of Leyden. They issued paper ordinances to feed starving thousands. Countless executions, wild hallucinations and prophetic frenzies all contributed to the reign of terror. Finally the opening of the city gates to their old oppressor, the bishop-prince, with complete extermination of every Anabaptist left in the city, was the horrible and tragic tale of the Munster experiment. Naturally, Winthrop and his associates wanted no such history repeated in Boston.

After a hundred years, this still hung over men's imaginations as a frightful possibility. Anabaptists had ceased to exist openly as a sect, though their ideas lived actively in many religious systems. The name, however, was a scare word and with it was linked the word Antino-mian. For more than one hundred and fifty years Munster continued to be held up as a horrible example. The Puritans were determined that no such ideas should penetrate to their cherished refuge in the New World, and they abhorred all variations from the accepted opinion as unstable, irresponsible, and destructive.

As a matter of fact, what the Antinomians really taught was that holiness consisted in a state of heart, not in good works. They upheld a Covenant of Grace based on a direct revelation in the individual soul of God's grace and love, rather than a Covenant of Works. This did not discourage a decent life, observance of the Sabbath, sobriety of dress and manner, but it did put all such good works in a subordinate place as the fruits rather than the proof of a believing heart. This was what Anne Hutchinson taught. It was what Governor Vane believed, and even Mr. Cotton lay under the suspicion of holding this opinion.

There have always been two theories about religion: one, that it is evidenced by externals, by forms, ceremonies and sacrifices, the other, that it is shown by conduct. It is the Law *vs.* the Gospel. The Puritans had revolted from the first and renounced forms and ceremonies. They based their hope of heaven on the injunction from Micah 6:8, "to do justly, and to love mercy, and to walk humbly before the Lord." Anne went still further, and taught that conduct was no test, that plain clothes, sober speech, and grave bearing were no evidence of Christianity, but that only one's inner life could testify to that.

Most confusing! How was the rest of that world to know? The poor Puritan fathers were naturally upset, especially when hundreds were joyfully accepting Anne's teaching.

All the Antinomians were under a suspicion of believing what indeed some of them did declare, that a believer could not sin, that whatever he did — provided he believed — he would be saved. The quaint defense offered by Captain Underhill for his loose conduct, though not strictly a fair example, indicated the way in which Antinomianism got its ill odor. The Captain testified that "he had been under a spirit of bondage and in a legal way five years, and could get no assurance; till at length as he was taking a pipe of tobacco, the Spirit sent home an absolute promise of free grace, with such assurance and joy as he never afterwards doubted of his good estate, neither should he, though he should fall into sin." So he trod the primrose path* with a good conscience.

The more the New England leaders thought about it, the more they were sure that Antinomianism was responsible for every kind of heresy. One offshoot of the Antinomians most horrifying to the Puritans was the Familists, who taught that all who loved Christ were bound together in a Family of Love, that it made no difference

---

* Primrose path: A path of ease or pleasure, especially sensual pleasure.

---

what one believed if only one was filled with a deep and all-pervading sense of divine love. That does not sound so dangerous now, but the orthodox Puritans had got the idea that free love was somehow mixed up with the theory. Then there were the Adamites, who wished to go clothed as Adam was in the Garden of Eden. Quite unsuited to a New England winter, there was little danger that this belief would prevail in Boston.

Winthrop, father of the colony, dreaded fanaticism of any sort. He knew that all these sects, even the mildest of them, believed in revelations, believed that God spoke to them directly as to the prophets of old. To his mind that was the most dangerous heresy conceivable. Revelation was finished. If not, who could tell where it would end, or what to believe? What was law and what was not law? The whole universe would be as shifting sand.

Anyone can see that a great many dangerous inferences could be drawn from the doctrine that a believing heart is the prime essential. It gave liberty in an age not prepared for it. There is something in the very nature of religious discussion that fosters strange and unexpected ideas and drives even cool and practical men to extremes. The founders of the colony were, for the most part, men of common sense and took no stock in fanaticism and far-fetched notions. The remembrance of the trouble they had taken to establish the colony and make it live through the terrible first summer was fresh in their minds. They had no intention of having their work undone by queer heresies. Though their intense religionism made them susceptible to extravagant doctrine, the English temperament helped to steady them. They might make religion their sole art and social diversion, but they devoted most of their working hours to grounding themselves sound and deep on an ample piece of New England soil. The Puritans had not scorned to take refuge, when it was necessary, in Holland, that stronghold of tolerance. However, they thought no more highly of that country on that account. Indeed, one of their writers describes Holland as "a mingle-mangle of religion, a cage of unclean birds where all sorts of strange religions flock as to a common harbor of heresies." John Winthrop and those who had labored most closely with him did not intend that the Massachusetts Bay Colony should be a refuge for any such motley crew.

Winthrop knew, also, that in order to keep their charter it was absolutely necessary to maintain a reputation for soundness and good order. He was extremely sensitive to the odor of religious controversy that clung to the colony. Hardly a year passed without some new tale being carried back to England about men whom they punished in Massachusetts for talking too freely. The story of Ratcliffe who had his ears cropped for blasphemy; of Henry Lyon whom they flogged on a similar charge; of Thomas Fox who had been set in the bilboes* for threatening to appeal to England; the story of the banishment of Roger Williams, all these lost nothing in transmission to the mother country. The prelatical party in England received every instance of disorder and religious dispute with a gleeful "I told you so."

Winthrop, as political leader of the colony as well as Winthrop the devout Puritan, feared and hated the Antinomians and the dissension that followed in their wake. So anxious were he and Wilson, and John Cotton as well, for the good repute of the colony that they implored those who were going back home to say nothing about the dispute. It is hard to see how they could have expected so exciting a scandal not to bubble forth from the lips of some gossiping traveler. Nevertheless, they hopefully made a plea for silence. Anne Hutchinson would not have been human if she had not been thrilled by the knowledge that when men and women went back to England they carried contraband news of her as the head of an influential faction in the New World. It could not very well have been

---

* Bilbo: a long bar of iron with sliding shackles used to confine the feet of prisoners, especially on shipboard.

---

disagreeable to her to realize that she had most of her own townspeople on her side and that the whole colony was discussing her and her works. Not Boston alone, but the surrounding towns were growing white-hot over the Covenant of Works and the Covenant of Grace.

To visitors at her meetings Anne patiently and graciously unfolded what she meant by the two terms. "In the beginning," she explained, "God made a covenant with Adam, giving the Earth to him on certain conditions. This was the Covenant of Works. Adam sinned and broke his part of the contract, so that the covenant was void. But God, instead of destroying him and his seed, made a new covenant with him whereby by His own Grace, He promised to save such as He should elect."

So far her hearers understood. This was good Calvinistic doctrine familiar to all of them. Anne went on.

"The old covenant is void. It is no more than the civil law. Under it no one can be saved. The elect are under the new Covenant of Grace."

"But how can I tell if I belong to God's elect?" each fevered soul demanded. That, after all, was the only thing that mattered. For this Anne had a test, as infallible and patent to her as it was intangible to some of her listeners.

"It is not by conduct, not by obeying the commandments, by giving alms, praying, fasting or wearing a long face. All that implies a mere Covenant of Works. Such things are good in themselves but they do not prove the state of one's heart, which alone counts. A serene spirit, coming from the consciousness of God's spirit within, proves to the true believer that he is among the elect. He in whom the Spirit dwells, he is of the elect."

"And he in whom it does not dwell — what of him?"

"Such a one may give all his goods to the poor, and his body be burned, if he has not the love of God in his heart, it profiteth nothing."

"Then how do we know which of our dear ones are to be saved?"

"No man knoweth the heart of another, save God alone. But each knoweth his own heart. Look for the light within."

"But Mr. Wilson preaches not so. He preaches the wearing of plain clothes, he preaches fasting and the avoidance of light conversation," objected her listener.

"True, Mr. Wilson preaches not so," replied Anne. "Two only in our whole colony preach the Covenant of Grace."

"And these two?"

"Mr. Cotton and my brother Wheelwright."

Of course this was at once reported to the other

ministers. They did not like it. The more they thought it over, the less they liked it and by the fall of 1636, jealous of their professional honor, they took the matter up with great warmth. In a flutter they came to Boston to find out what Anne Hutchinson meant. One by one they made their way to the house at the corner of Market Street and Sentry Lane, and each privately asked its mistress if she meant him. Gently, but firmly, she said she did. Why not? She truly thought that each questioner was seeking information in all honesty and that the truth would free him of his error.

It was while these things were going on that Anne broached her plan to have Wheelwright appointed a teacher in the Boston church, was frustrated, and saw him settled in Wollaston. At almost the same time came the flurry over Vane's resignation.

After this, events followed thick and fast.

On the one hand, the Boston church very nearly went to the extremity of admonishing Pastor Wilson in open meeting for having ventured to criticize "the opinions that have arisen in our midst." Cotton prevented this unprecedented action, then, nevertheless, gravely exhorted his colleague. Poor Mr. Wilson had the humiliation of seeing his church all but wrested away from him by the popularity of Anne Hutchinson's lectures. It speaks well for both Wilson and Cotton that they managed to stay friends throughout all this turmoil. However, Wilson inevitably liked Anne Hutchinson less and less. He staved off a calamity by preaching a sermon that did not give offense. Vane generously praised it in front of the congregation, and Wilson hung on.

On the other hand, the clergy throughout the colony were galled at having been lumped together by the lady lecturer as preachers of nothing but a Covenant of Works. They decided it was high time to take some steps about it. First they must know what Mr. Cotton really thought and whether he was actually, as had been asserted, the fountainhead of the Hutchinson opinions. So they met and drew up sixteen points for him to explain, but neither he nor they were any better off for his answers.

In February, while strife was waxing hotter and hotter, a ship was about to sail for England. Both Cotton and Wilson felt anxious that the travelers should carry back to England a good report of the serenity of the colony, and to this end each preached a sermon intended to smooth matters over. The effect, says Winthrop, was to clear the subject up "so no man could tell (except some few who knew the bottom of the matter) where any difference was."

Such a superficial adjustment could not serve for long, because at the bottom were the wounded feelings of the clergymen whom Anne had unfavorably compared with her chosen Cotton and Wheelwright. She had said it. She admitted it. Gently, but remorselessly, she admitted it, and nothing could allay the sting except wholesale retraction. Retraction was the furthest from her thought.

"Thus every occasion," wrote Winthrop, "increased the contention, and carried great alienation of minds; and the members of Boston (frequenting the lectures of other ministers) did make much disturbance by public questions, and the objections to their doctrines; and it began to be as common here to distinguish between men, by being under a covenant of grace or a covenant of works, as in other countries between Protestant and Papist."

The spirit of discord was now at its height. Anne was holding the reins of a runaway horse. All that winter of 1637, throughout the colony, went the clack, clack of tongues. The people could not dance, they could not go to a play, they had no music worth mentioning, they had no books except those of a terrifying dullness, but they could talk — *and talk they did.* Perhaps it kept them warm. (That was the winter when their convenient stock of firewood began to fail.) Still, no fire spreads so quickly as a church quarrel and the wind of gossip was blowing the flame to its height. Most voluble and most bitter of all the talkers were the women coming home from Anne's meetings. The women had not found such a relish in life since the time they left England. *But Anne was feeling the thorns in her crown of leadership.*

"The Antinomian Controversy" nearly broke up the colony, but much of its destructive power lay in the imaginary terrors of the name.

XI

THE ATTACK STRENGTHENS

Anne's failure to establish Wheelwright in the Boston church was a bitter disappointment. This was not simply because it was her project and her brother-in-law, though probably anyone and anything that belonged to her possessed special merit in her eyes. It was also because he preached what she believed. Moreover, she was sure that Mr. Wilson was a detriment to the Boston church and she had hoped to offset his influence. She had on her mind those dear souls who had so often confided their troubles to her, whose hearts she had lightened a little with her gentler teaching. On these hearts, like a blighting frost, fell the stern, legalized preaching of Wilson, delivered with heavy, harsh voice and dogmatic manner. Wilson was an admirable man, devoted to his people, spending his fortune freely in the service of the colony. However, he lacked the persuasiveness and personal magnetism that were the great assets of his colleague Cotton and of Anne Hutchinson. It was not his fault that he had embraced a more austere doctrine; it was his misfortune that to most of his parishioners at this time it was not acceptable. Anne felt personally responsible for those who had sought her counsel, and she had trusted to her influence to bring more congenial preaching into the church. With Cotton and Wheelwright both preaching the Gospel of Grace, they would minimize the effect of Wilson's sermons. Perhaps she would have stopped there, but probably she would have been glad to see him go. Wilson himself was convinced that she was actually working to oust him, and he was fighting for his standing in the community and for his job.

Wilson had won the first engagement. Through her lieutenants Anne had been defeated. They did not appoint Wheelwright. Governor Vane was out of favor. Cotton, insofar as he took sides, was still with her, but all of them together had not been able to override Wilson when Winthrop backed him.

They had settled the matter tactfully. Wheelwright and all the Hutchinsonians made the best of his appointment to the new chapel at Mount Wollaston. There he preached for a year and was well liked. He probably held his services in a farmhouse that William Coddington had built on the great estate granted to him and his friend Edmund Quincy. Thither Coddington and other Bostonians would retire over the weekend to listen to Wheelwright.

It was a tempestuous year for Wheelwright, because during that time the General Court tried and banished him on the ground of sedition. Although he had to spend so much of his time before the Court and got himself so talked about, Wollaston never failed him. Wheelwright was a born fighter, an aggressive man without much tact, but sincere and so admitted by his worst enemies. His first year in Boston was worse than anything he had experienced in his wanderings about England. The truth is, he found his sister-in-law more radical than he had expected her to be.

Anne's failure in the Wheelwright affair did not lessen her popularity in Boston. They still thronged her meetings. As one of her contemporaries, Robert Keayne, best known as the first commander of the Ancient and Honorable Artillery Company, expressed it, "She had a fluent tongue and a forwardness in Expressions to seduce and draw away many, Espetilly those of her own sex." There was a great fluttering of letters back and forth between Winthrop and Cotton on Mr. Wilson's account. Many of them were made public, copies were circulated, and tongues wagged more than ever. "Loving and gentle and plain" were the letters, according to Winthrop, and the plainness more than anything else must have given great joy to the readers. It was partly these letters, passing round from one hand to another, that spread the controversy to the neighboring towns. The other ministers sympathized devoutly with Mr. Wilson for the trouble he was having in his church. They sympathized a hundredfold more because they were tarred with the same brush by the same hand. That impertinent woman was saying that there were only two ministers in New England — in all New England, if you please — who preached a Covenant of Grace. All the others were mere legalists, sealed with a Covenant of Works.

The ministers were angry for the good reason that the shoe pinched. They very well knew that they were preaching such a covenant. Then why be so put out about it? Because one woman could not abide their preaching, indeed!

"A company of legal professors lie poring on the law which Christ hath abolished," she said.

Two of the ministers long since knew and distrusted her opinions — Symmes of Charlestown (whose son later married her granddaughter), and Lothrop of Salem, her erstwhile fellow travelers. Thomas Weld of Roxbury also, having submitted his preaching to her test and failed to please her, never forgave her. We can say this for the ministers, that she had touched them in their tenderest part, their pride in their preaching. Here they were, proud to serve God to the best of their powers, interpreters of God's law to their people. And, here was this woman, questioning their doctrine, their preaching, nay, even their very right to a place among God's elect. They could not understand her at all except that she seemed to consider herself inspired. *Religion was a matter of life and death to all of them. Yet they were sober enough, middle-class Englishmen that they were, to keep their feet on the ground and avoid the metaphysical. This woman was a mystic. She was what they called an "Enthusiast," using the word in its original Greek sense of one inspired, one into whose soul a god had breathed. However, the ministers meant not one who was inspired, but one who **thought** he was inspired. They knew that they were not inspired — why should William Hutchinson's good lady be?* They all felt profoundly sorry for Brother Wilson.

Being gentlemen, they did not strike at a lady, not at first. Their immediate desire was to find out where Cotton really stood and, if possible, win him over to their side. Therefore, they began a campaign of letter writing especially directed to Cotton, and he, ready letter-writer that he was, made haste to answer them. Throughout the fall and winter of 1636-37, the principal indoor sport in the colony of Massachusetts was the writing and reading of ministerial letters. The best person was he who got the latest bulletin. Those who failed to see the letters heard about them Sunday when the preachers used them as material for their sermons. Lieutenant-Governor Thomas Hutchinson, sketching the career of his great-great-grandmother one hundred and forty years later, wrote: "The fear of God and love of their neighbor seemed laid by and out of the question."

Early that winter they held a meeting that was of the gravest consequence to Anne Hutchinson. The ministers of the colony, hearing that she had compared them with Cotton to their own disadvantage, conferred with him. They wanted to know just what the difference was. They wanted, in case Cotton held unorthodox views, to reclaim him; they certainly wanted to vindicate themselves. Therefore, they sought a conference with him and suggested that it be held in the presence of the magistrates.

Cotton replied that it was not so much a matter for magistrates as for the lady who made the criticism. Therefore, it would be well to talk it over with her. Perhaps he thought that by bringing the disgruntled clergy and their critic together, they might accomplish an understanding. He was skilled at compromise.

The conference did not work out as Cotton intended. For Anne it was calamitous.

Fragmentary reports of the meeting have been handed down. They held it in Cotton's house. The ministers from the village churches came in, among them the robustious but public-spirited Hugh Peter, who had taken Roger William's place at Salem. Also, the stubborn Zachariah Symmes of Charlestown, the delicate Thomas Shepard of Newtowne, Weld of Roxbury, Phillips of Watertown, Ward of Ipswich, John Wilson, of course, and John Wheelwright attended. The Governor was there, Leverett, ruling elder of the Boston church, was there, and most of the magistrates. John Cotton greeted them all with his smiling hospitality, and then ushered in the lady.

Her entrance had an electric quality. Her clear-cut features, her proud carriage, her decisiveness, produced an effect, as it always did, even before she opened her mouth to speak. The impetuous Hugh Peter took upon himself the office of the spokesman. However, before he embarked upon his subject, Governor Vane, mindful of the far-reaching consequences that this conference might have, suggested that a written record of the meeting be made. On his recommendation Pastor Wilson was chosen secretary.

Mr. Peter then proceeded. With his usual vehemence he besought Anne Hutchinson to explain in what way he and his brother-ministers differed from Mr. Cotton. He had heard that she had made it her table talk that they preached a Covenant of Works, while Cotton alone, with

Mr. Wheelwright, taught a Covenant of Grace. Was that true?

At first she considered the standing of her questioners and tried to spare their feelings. It was hard, face to face with them, to tell them what she thought of their preaching, at least those with whom she had had no personal quarrel. She had never even met some of them before. As graciously as she could, she returned an evasive answer.

But her interrogator was not to be put off. In his excitement, he pressed the question and hotly quoted words she had been said to utter.

It seemed to Anne that a plain duty lay here. No doubt the ministers were seeking light in all honesty. Here was a chance to be of service. A coward she would be and unfaithful to her trust if she did not bear witness to the truth. "The fear of man is a snare," she thought. "Why should I be afraid?" Why, indeed, when fear was so far from her habit?

With this inner heartening she spoke out. Yes, she said there was a difference between them and Mr. Cotton. Mr. Cotton preached a Covenant of Grace; they preached a Covenant of Works.

Who, for instance, had preached a Covenant of Works?

Well, Mr. Shepard, she thought did not preach a Covenant of Grace quite as clearly as Mr. Cotton did.

Neither did Mr. Weld, though both gave fine discourses.

Why? — the unfortunate gentlemen thus singled out for notice wanted to know — why did they not preach a Covenant of Grace?

"You can preach no more than you know," she said sweetly. "It is like the Apostles before the resurrection of Christ, before they were sealed with the seal of the Spirit."

What did she mean by "being sealed with the seal of the Spirit"?

Well, there was the broad seal and the little seal. The broad seal was the seal of the Spirit, the full assurance of God's favor by the Holy Spirit. The little seal — but here the explanation ran off into metaphysics beyond the power of any to comprehend.

The Reverend George Phillips of Watertown thought he would catch the lady in a trap. What did she think of his preaching, how did it differ from Brother Cotton's? He asked, knowing well that she had never heard him.

Her answer was positive. She had heard of him, and his preaching — she hated to say it, but she could not be a shirker — his preaching, too, was not sealed — not as Mr. Cotton's was.

Cotton was uncomfortable. It was not working out at all as he had hoped. He was especially embarrassed to be compared in this fashion with his fellow ministers. It might be best to close the conference before she said anything worse. So, with kindly words about the honor of being likened to the Apostles, whether before or after the Resurrection, Cotton pleasantly dismissed the assembly and accompanied his guests to the door. They departed, divided in their minds, hardly knowing what they thought. Cotton's good humor and the lady's charm hypnotized them for the moment into believing that they had not been so badly treated. Only Mr. Weld lingered. Just why, no one knows; perhaps he was going to spend the night. At any rate, while Cotton talked with the others at the door, Weld and Anne Hutchinson held converse by the window.

On the conference between Anne and the ministers and in part, on her conversation with Weld, hinged her trial before the Court fifteen months later. As to what she really said, they differed among themselves, and Wilson unfortunately did not keep his notes. On one point they agreed as they thought it over, namely, that this self-appointed critic had declared that they were not able ministers of the Gospel. In their agitation they could not let the subject rest, and some of them "singly went with tears to her," to find out if she really meant what she said. "Do you mean me?" each of them insisted. She left them no room for doubt, and their sense of insult resolved itself into a slowly growing grudge.

When the Court met in January, the ministers left their pulpits for three weeks and came to Boston to talk it over at greater length. By this time, the smoke of battle had grown very sweet in Anne's nostrils. Party lines were drawn more sharply than ever, with Cotton, Wheelwright, Vane, and all the Boston church, except a stubborn four or five, on Anne's side. On the other side, stood all the rest of the Massachusetts ministers and Winthrop. Winthrop and Cotton, who both thought that there might be some compromise, were aghast at the turmoil. The rest, whether on one side or the other, were diehards and showed no signs of reluctance at entering the fray.

An attack on John Wheelwright evidenced the first stage in the decline of Anne's influence. January 20 was set apart by the General Court as a day of fasting for all the churches. "The occasion was," says Winthrop, "the miserable state of the churches in Germany, the calamities upon our native land, the bishops making havock in the churches, putting down the faithful ministers, and advancing popish ceremonies and doctrines, the plague raging exceedingly, and famine and sword threatening them; the dangers of those in Connecticut, and of ourselves also, by the Indians; and the dissensions in our churches."

It was characteristic of seventeenth-century writing

that he put the chief reason for the fast at the end. However, Winthrop and the colony were probably worried over the other things, too.

They held the fast as decreed. In the Boston church that afternoon Cotton preached first, then Wheelwright, on Cotton's invitation.

Wheelwright's sermon, preserved from shorthand notes taken by Robert Keayne, sounds mild enough after more than three centuries. It caused little disturbance at the time, but later, when the controversy reached still more bitter heights, it did his enemies good service.

As the winter progressed, the ill will between the two factions kept growing more acrimonious. Boston members persisted in going about to the lectures of the other ministers, rising in church to question the preacher and to expound their own doctrine. All who were able-bodied got out to Anne's double-weekly lecture. Even those who had to keep to their houses could still talk.

In Boston itself, Anne's magnetic presence and the gratitude felt for her charities still prevailed. However, in the outlying towns her popularity was fading with that of Vane. Into a theological quarrel between the clergy and a critical, outspoken woman there had entered a political complication on Vane's account, that made men like Dudley, and even Winthrop, think it best to force an issue.

By the time the General Court convened in March, there was a strong sentiment against Vane and any opinions that Vane might advocate. Still, the season was not yet quite ripe for striking at him. That could wait for the May meeting when they would vote for governor. For the present they found a scapegoat in Wheelwright and an issue in that Fast Day sermon of his. They called him before the Court and bid him to give account for what he had said that day.

At first, the Court meant to hold his examination in private. However, some Boston members objected that private examinations smacked of Laud's High Commission proceedings. After a second complaint and Wheelwright's stubborn refusal to answer questions put to him privately, the magistrates and ministers were determined to secure a verdict of sedition and contempt. Nevertheless, they had a hard struggle to do it, especially since Vane, the presiding officer, was against it. Vane protested everything that he could, but the Court would not allow his protests to stand.

Anne was not idle and rallied her supporters to the defense of her brother-in-law. This defense reached its climax in the famous Boston Petition, a document signed by sixty members of the Boston church. All that it did was to deny, in moderate terms, that there was anything seditious in Wheelwright's Fast Day sermon. However, the Petition was afterwards used against the sixty signers to their very great hurt. Incidentally, it produced no effect on Wheelwright's trial.

Finally, the Court rendered their decision.

Anne Hutchinson, hearing it, must have felt a premonition of her own fate. The vote was that Wheelwright's sermon, though not *intended* to cause disturbance, *tended* to do so, and they therefore judged him guilty of sedition. The Court put off deciding his punishment until their next meeting, in order that he might have a chance to retract.

One other motion passed that day showed Anne beyond a shadow of a doubt that the prestige of her friend the Governor was waning. They voted that they should hold the spring election in Newtowne, now Cambridge, rather than in Boston. This was a move on the part of the clerical element to minimize the influence of the Boston voters and increase that of those from the outside towns, which were anti-Hutchinsonian. Vane, as presiding officer, refused to put the motion, but it was put by Endicott and carried.

The effect of this meeting of the Court was greatly to intensify the strife. The Boston church considered that it had been insulted in having its Petition rejected. Anne no longer made any effort to endure Mr. Wilson's preaching.   Even before this she had often frankly questioned the doctrine of his sermons; worse yet, she had ostentatiously walked out of meeting as soon as he rose to preach. Now she could not bring herself to sit under him any longer and she established what was practically a church of her own in her own house.

The Puritan was dimly groping after the idea that the court of last appeal for himself was his own conscience. However, he could not yet see any reason for granting the same privilege to other men. Nevertheless, the right of liberty of thought was being formulated. In this same year, 1637, a great French philosopher, taking refuge in Holland, propounded in his "Method of Reasoning and Investigating Scientific Truth," the theory that thought should be untrammeled. At the same time, a merchant's wife in a primitive New England village and René Descartes, alike insisted "that the conscious judgment of the mind is its highest authority."

XII

THE MAY ELECTION

Anne was now in the thick of a fight that concerned, not only the reputation of her dearest friends, but their very continuance in the colony. Her lieutenant, Wheelwright, was under conviction for sedition. Although they had given him a chance to retract, she knew full well that he would not do so. That light had gone out so far as Boston was concerned. Her political and social ally, Governor Vane, also walked under a cloud that was constantly growing blacker and blacker; even while presiding at a public meeting of the General Court, they had overridden and set him aside. John Cotton, her third defense, was keeping himself safe from direct censure only by his moderation and his unfailing gift for the answer that turns away wrath.

Her mind was anxiously set on the May election when the governor, deputy-governor, and magistrates were to be chosen. It behooved her party to secure what advantage they could while Vane was in power, and to take care that the Boston delegation be as strong as possible. She was quite aware of the shrewd blow struck at Vane when they appointed the place of meeting for the spring election at

Newtowne instead of Boston. The voters of the outlying towns were not on her side, except in the case of the comparatively small number of her personal acquaintances. If she could only see them and talk with them, if they would all come to her meetings, she felt sure that she could win them over. Yet try as hard as she might, she had neither strength nor time to minister to the whole colony.

So Anne dreaded the May election. She foresaw that it would be packed with voters from the unfriendly towns on the west side of the Charles River. She knew that her own adherents, except the more ardent among them, might be kept away by the troublesome trip. For this she must encourage her auxiliaries and pray for good weather.

All the variances and animosities in the colony were centered on Anne and her friends. The jealousy that existed between Boston and the other towns, the clash between Wheelwright and the rest of the clergy, the more stubborn though less clearly defined antagonism between the impetuous young Governor and older men like Winthrop and Dudley, even the friction between the colony and the home government — all focused on Anne and the Hutchinson faction. Anne's friends were always together on one side. Anne's doctrine was the wedge that widened each division.

In addition to the open ruptures, there was something more subtle and all-pervading. Among the common people there was stirring faintly an antagonism against the magistrates, a lurking satisfaction in seeing them get the worst of an argument, a class consciousness, unacknowledged by the rulers and inarticulate on the part of the common people, but potent. Many of Anne's most loyal supporters were among the poorer members of the colony, to whose women she had ministered. She almost pitied them for their loyalty, for she suspected that they understood very little of the doctrine involved. They were the bitterest of all against Mr. Wilson and the most ardent for her, making the matter a personal issue as is the habit of the man in the street.

Most penetrating and inclusive of all the differences was that between those who rested their hope of salvation on a good heart and those who rested it on good deeds. On that ground everyone took a stand, whether he knew anything about theology or not, and it was for Anne that they were all named, friends and enemies, Hutchinsonians or anti-Hutchinsonians. There seemed to be room on middle ground for no one except John Cotton. The rest of the colony was either for her or against her.

Was she glad or sorry to be at the center of such strife? Consciously, neither. She was so intent upon all the ramifications of the controversy and so busy getting things done to help Wheelwright and Vane that she did not knowingly consider the bearing of it all upon herself. Subconsciously, of course, it exhilarated her. She was in that state so familiar to her in a crisis, where everything made a sharper impression upon her senses and produced a quickening of her powers. It was a time when everything was of consequence to her except the actual consequences. What it would mean to her and to her family in the end did not enter into her calculations.

The two months between the March meeting of the General Court and the May election saw Anne and her friends very busy. They prepared to defend Wheelwright, marshaled their forces and looked to their ammunition. For Anne it was far different from being on the crest of the wave, as she had been a year before. In the bustle of her preparations for Wheelwright's defense she hardly noticed how much things had changed for her personally.

The first move made by the Hutchinsonians was to revive the Petition signed by sixty members of the Boston church and presented at the former meeting of the Court. At that time the Court had turned the Petition down as "groundless and presumptuous," and then, seemingly, forgotten it. Now Anne Hutchinson and Vane, with Coddington and others, decided that the Petition ought to be put before the whole people at the May election. It was a form of modern referendum that they sought to institute. To make sure that the Petition would be brought up, they determined to introduce it before the election of officers, when they feared that Vane might be put out of office. Under the guise of business left over from the previous meeting they hoped to slip it in first.

When Election Day arrived, it was fine enough to suit even fair-weather voters. The date was the 17th of May, the 27th by the present calendar,* and a perfect forerunner of summer. At one o'clock the voters gathered around a big oak on the north side of a great field that is now Cambridge Common. The boy Governor, standing an elegant, slim, urban figure in those rural surroundings under the open sky, called the meeting to order. The first business, he announced, was to take action on a petition sent from the Boston church on behalf of Mr. John Wheelwright.

The referendum got no chance. Instantly John Winthrop was on his feet objecting that the Petition was out of order. "This meeting," he said, "has been called

---

* Great Britain did not change from the Julian calendar to the Gregorian calendar until 1752, which required an increase of ten days to restore the next equinox to its proper date.

for the election of officers. That is the business before the assembly, and that business must be disposed of first." Vane insisted, and an angry debate followed.

Some of the voters had come to blows amid shouts of "Petition!" and "Election!" and the meeting was getting quite out of the control of the youthful presiding officer. In the midst of the tumult, John Wilson used his powerful voice to good purpose for his cause. In spite of his fifty years and his portly build, he seized the lower branches of the oak tree and drew himself up above the excited throng. He cried out loudly to them, "Freemen, look to your charter!" At this, the majority of the voters shouted to go on with the election. However, Vane was still set on getting the Petition before them and refused to open the polls. At last Winthrop, who was the next official in rank, said they would proceed to the election anyway, and Vane had to give in.

Picture Anne, that warm May evening, watching by her open door for her husband to return with news of the election. As at last she saw him coming up the road, she did not need his gesture of negation to corroborate the story told by his discouraged air and weary step.

"Not one?" she asked.

Again he turned his hand down.

"Who are in power, then?"

"Mr. Winthrop as Governor, Thomas Dudley as deputy."

"And the magistrates? Surely Mr. Vane is one of them!"

"Not even that. All our friends are out. Coddington, Hough, Dummer, every one of them."

"Well, I expected that," said Anne calmly. "What of the Petition?"

"That, too. Winthrop objected and some of them cried down the Governor when he tried to read it."

"That was shameful!" she flashed. "To hold him in such disesteem! What more did they do?"

"That is all, except that they voted Mr. John Endicott a magistrate for life."

"'Tis against our charter!" she cried in anger.

"Ay, what of that? They did it before for Winthrop and Dudley."

The effect of this defeat on Anne and the more energetic of her party was to make them work harder than ever. Those whom the colony had delighted to honor were cast down; Vane, Coddington, and Hough were not even magistrates. Endicott, foe of all heretics, was magistrate for life, Winthrop and Dudley were at the head of the government. Before another day dawned the leaders of the opposition in Boston met and planned their next move. It was to indicate, by the choice of their deputies to the General Court, their resentment at the course of the election. The deputies that Boston elected were the very men who had been dropped from the magistracy, Vane, Coddington, and Hough.

The Court immediately retaliated by declaring the Boston election illegal on the ground that two voters had somehow failed to receive a warrant of the meeting. So the Boston voters met again and stubbornly returned the same men. This election was allowed to stand for the time being, but these three were the only Hutchinsonians in the entire General Court. Politically, Anne's friends were out.

There now ensued a confused and somewhat childish interchange of reprisals. The halberdiers who habitually escorted Governor Vane to church, being Boston men and one of them brother Edward Hutchinson, now refused to perform a similar service for Winthrop. On Sunday Vane and Coddington ostentatiously gave up their usual seats of honor with the magistrates and sat with the deacons. When they summoned Boston to supply her quota for the Pequot War, not a church member responded. They alleged that they did not care to serve with a chaplain who preached a Covenant of Works, none other than their own pastor, John Wilson. So much on the Hutchinson side.

On the other hand, one of the first acts of the new General Court was to pass an immigration law. They called it the Exclusion Act, to the effect that no town could receive any person for a longer time than three weeks without permission from one of the Governor's Council or two of the magistrates. That meant that no one could settle in Massachusetts without permission from Winthrop, Dudley, Endicott, or two of their eight associates. The special purport of this law was against some of Anne's friends and relatives who were on their way to America. These arrived in July, among them Samuel Hutchinson, William's brother. They were respectable, God-fearing men and women and they certainly expected to be welcome when they disembarked after their uncomfortable voyage. But no! They could not buy a piece of land, they could not be the guests of their friends for more than three weeks unless the magistrates gave consent. The magistrates did not give consent, believing them, with good cause, to be Hutchinsonian. In consideration of the fact that they had left England before the law was passed, they were allowed four months' grace. Then they had to go. It is supposed that they toiled on to Exeter, New Hampshire.

It may have been during this session of the Court that John Winthrop's wife put a sweet and charitable letter into his hands:

"Dear in my thoughts,

I blush to think how much I have neglected the opportunity of presenting my love to you. Sad thoughts possess my spirits, and I cannot repulse them, which makes me unfit for anything, wondering what the Lord means by all these troubles among us. Sure I am, that all shall work out to the best of them that Love God, or rather are loved of Him. I know He will bring light out of obscurity, and make His righteousness shine forth as clear as the noon day. Yet I find in myself an adverse spirit, and a trembling heart, not so well to submit to the will of God as I desire. There is a time to plant, and a time to pull up that which is planted, which I could desire might not be yet. But the Lord knoweth what is best, and His will be done. But I will write no more. Hoping to see thee tomorrow, my best affections being commended to yourself, the rest of our friends at Newton, I commend thee to God.

Your loving Wife,
Margaret Winthrop."

Sad Boston, 1637.

Truly a humane and tender letter to a worried husband whom she hopes to see on the morrow! Gentlest of all is the passage, "There is . . . a time to pull up that which is planted, *which I could desire might not be yet.*"

Was Winthrop's own house a house divided?

The Exclusion Act stirred the people up more than anything else. Vane attacked its validity but Winthrop defended it, and it stood. Vane also encouraged Wheelwright to appeal his case to the King, but the Massachusetts Court refused to allow any appeal. Soon after that, when a Fast Day was appointed in the colony, Vane and Coddington, instead of going to hear Mr. Wilson preach at their own church, went down to Wollaston to listen to Wheelwright. Everybody got crosser and crosser, except perhaps John Cotton and John Winthrop.

Winthrop sought to find a dignified way out of the tangle by suggesting to Vane that he and his friends form a new colony somewhere else. He even went so far as to send word to Roger Williams, asking if these other troublemakers of the Massachusetts Colony might join him in his retreat at Providence. If they had accepted Winthrop's diplomatic suggestion at once, they would have saved a great deal of trouble for themselves and others.

At this point nineteen-year-old Lord Ley, son of the Earl of Marlborough, came over on a sight-seeing tour. In his honor Governor Winthrop gave a dinner party, but the guest of honor did not attend. Instead of that, he let

Vane take him down to Noddle's Island where Mr. Samuel Maverick still persisted in dispensing the genial hospitality of Merry England in spite of Boston censorship. The excuse Vane gave to Winthrop for not attending the gubernatorial dinner was that his conscience withheld him, which hardly seems a courteous way of expressing regret. What excuse Lord Ley, a well-mannered youth, gave is not recorded.

When Lord Ley returned to England, Vane went with him, and glad he was to go. A great concourse of Hutchinsonians came down to see him off. Some of them even rowed out to the ship. They fired off their arms in salute and the guns at Castle Island voiced their respect. Governor Winthrop did not attend in person to wish the two highborn youths godspeed, but he did give the order to have the salute fired. Thus, everybody's dignity was saved.

Departing, Vane had spoken plainly for religious toleration: "Scribes and Pharisees, and such as are confirmed in any way of error, all such are not to be denied cohabitation but are to be pitied and reformed. Ishmael shall dwell in the presence of his brethren."

Vane did not show to the best advantage in America. Partly because the people, carried away by the glamor of his rank and personal charms, thrust upon him political honors for which he was not ready. Yet Winthrop, who suffered some slights on his account, had the magnanimity to admire the same quality in Vane. Winthrop wrote, "Although he might have taken occasion against us for some dishonor, which he apprehended to have been unjustly put upon him here, yet he showed himself at all times as true friend to New England and a man of noble and generous mind."

In the desperate days in England that followed the death of Oliver Cromwell, Vane was first a member of the Committee of Safety and then President of the Council. He proved himself far in advance of his time and yet practical enough to have accomplished his dream of a republic, had not General Monk sold the army to Prince Charles. In Massachusetts Vane was ahead of his time. Winthrop, more politic, perhaps a man of smaller caliber, but patient, attentive to detail and unsparing in personal labor for the colony, could do more to establish it on a firm foundation because he shared the opinions, and the prejudices, of the more influential men. Although they might be carried away by Vane's charm and lineage for a time, and although they never got over liking to show Winthrop their power once in a while, they would follow him longer than they would Vane.

As for Anne, she never ceased to mourn the loss of

that bright spirit, so accoutered with the draperies of earthly and celestial glory. Vane was everything she could have wished a son of her own to have been — the dream-child that every woman has.

Between the two there was one of those friendships that sometimes exist between an older, maternal woman and a very young man. A friendship untouched by passion, but founded, for his part, on the security that he feels in being able to pour out his thoughts to a woman without being suspected of sentiment, and for her part, on the delight that any woman takes in being guide to a charming youth. Added to this was the fact that Anne Hutchinson provided Vane with intelligent conversation, and that he helped to create for her an air of social prestige.

Above all, was the sympathy of their spirits, their common impulse toward the higher life. Anne missed her young friend with a yearning that was never assuaged.

XIII

THE SYNOD

W hen Vane left Boston in early August, Anne lost her strongest civil supporter. At the end of the same month came an event that showed what she could expect of her spiritual adviser, John Cotton. In still another six weeks, they ordered that her fellow worker Wheelwright leave the colony.

On the 30th of August they held the first Council of the Congregational Churches in America. They called it the Synod. The clergy organized it for the purpose of bringing the Antinomian controversy to a head, giving Wheelwright a chance to retract, and proving where Cotton stood. The ministers were armed and girded to rout out all heresies, clean up the colony, and vindicate themselves as "able ministers."

Anne recognized perfectly that she was on the eve of a battle, but she felt no fear for herself. By this time, she was so upon her mettle that she welcomed each new aspect of the strife. The very fact that she was shorn of the support of Vane, that dear John Cotton was acting as if he had something on his mind, that Brother Wheelwright was momentarily expecting sentence, gave her buoyancy. She felt as if she alone, unaided, could uphold the doctrines she had taught. Her feeling was exactly that which produces martyrs, a feeling stupendous and inescapable that urges one to witness for the faith.

For the colony in general, the summer had brought some toning down of the excitement. The people, busy about their farms, cared less about covenants. In New England the winter has always been the season for self-improvement and propaganda. This summer of 1637 happened to be unusually hot. So hot that Governor Winthrop returning from the North Shore had to travel by night. Too hot for violent championship of causes or persons.

Thanks to the good offices of Hooker and some of the other ministers, they had patched up a reconciliation between Cotton and Wilson. Wilson said that, when he had referred in meeting to the "opinions" that were upsetting his church, he had not meant any advocated from the pulpit by Messrs. Cotton and Wheelwright. He had been referring to opinions held privately by various members of the church. Whereupon hearing this, Mr. Cotton generously exonerated Mr. Wilson of any intention to offend. The next Sunday, the elders of the Boston church, hitherto on edge to censure their pastor, withdrew their charges. "This sudden change," says Winthrop, who was Wilson's constant friend, "was much observed by some" (meaning himself) because Wilson had previously offered the same excuses to both elders and congregation without softening their animosity. The fact that the church was now willing to accept Wilson's explanation might have shown Anne that several of her friends were weakening. Nevertheless, by this time she was hoping against hope.

Another occurrence that helped to make Boston better disposed toward Wilson was the successful outcome of the Pequot War. Although Wilson had gone along as chaplain, his Covenant of Works had evidently done the expedition no harm. They had defeated the Pequots with great slaughter while Massachusetts lost only one man "and that by a flux," had only one other disabled and that with the asthma that he carried with him. Bostonians began to say that perhaps after all God had guided the drawing of the lot that gave the chaplaincy to Wilson. At any rate, God had not blasted him or his spiritual charges for the Covenant of Works, as some had gloomily foretold.

This softening of public opinion in Boston toward Wilson had two results. One was to tempt Anne's more ardent adherents to lose their heads and resort to "hot speeches, violent words and a fever of anger." The other was to encourage her opponents in the colony at large to bring the controversy to an open and definite issue. Therefore, with the determination of removing what Thomas Weld calls "that fearfull leprosy," the ministers and magistrates agreed to call a synod, to meet at Newtowne, August 30, 1637.

About twenty-five ministers with lay delegates and magistrates were present in an official capacity. By vote of the General Court, Massachusetts paid all expenses of delegates outside the colony. The meetings were open to the public. Surely Anne, so vitally concerned in the deliberations, made every effort to attend.

Newtowne was at this time a village of sixty or seventy cabins. Hooker's congregation had vacated the cabins when they went to Connecticut and sold them to the parishioners of Thomas Shepard who arrived at about the same time. The church where they held the meetings was a bleak little building of bare boards, standing where Dunster Street now joins Mr. Auburn Street. In front of it ran the main road of the village down to the Charles. Nearby was Dudley's house. South was the river, north was a broad, level plain, then used for common pasturage. Here stood the great oak where Vane had met his defeat. To the south of the oak, Harvard College was soon to be built.

The Synod opened with a prayer by Shepard, a minister

who fell only a very little short of Anne Hutchinson's requirements in grace. He is described as being at this time "a poore, weake, pale-complectioned man of 34, holy, heavenly, sweet-affecting and soul-ravishing." Bulkley of Concord and Hooker of Connecticut were chosen moderators. They hired John Higginson to take shorthand notes of the proceedings. The conference lasted twenty-four days; it was a twenty-four day controversial dissipation.

The first business was to read a paper prepared by some of the ministers. They had set down all the unorthodox opinions that they had found flying about the colony. It was an appalling list, containing eighty-two so-called heresies and nine "unwholesome expressions." Among them Anne heard many of her own words repeated, but along with them strange vagaries that she had never even imagined. One minister, aghast at the swarm of heterodoxies, cried out after the reading, "What is to be done with them?" John Wilson vigorously replied, "Let them all go to the devil of hell whence they came!"

First the Synod wanted to debate each item; at the outset, in writing, then since this took too much time, in extemporaneous debate from the floor. *Everybody could take part, but "everybody" did not mean women. Anne had to keep silent.*

The Boston delegation protested, with some justice, that talking about the errors gave them undue publicity. However, if they must discuss them then let the names of those who held them be given. The ministers replied that it was not persons but doctrine that concerned them. The adherents of Anne Hutchinson, however, kept making themselves obnoxious by calling for witnesses. Finally, the magistrates told them that if they did not keep still they would be arrested for disturbing the peace. "Magistrates have nothing to do with a church meeting," they objected. "Try it and see," the magistrates retorted.

Upon that, some of the Boston men departed from the assembly and came no more. The ministers were then unhampered.

The debate went on with ecclesiastical fervor and prodigality of expression for more than three weeks. Anne Hutchinson, looking on in the company of those of her friends who remained, heard blow after blow struck at her, her conduct, and her beliefs, though she was not called by name. The Council decided that women's meetings were disorderly. A few might gather to pray and edify one another, "yet such a set assembly (as was in practice at Boston) where sixty or more did meet every week, and one woman (in a prophetical way, by resolving questions of doctrine and expounding Scripture) took upon her the whole exercise, was agreed to be disorderly and without rule." This was Blow Number One!

The Council also decided that questions and discussions at the close of a sermon were out of order. A private member might ask information, wisely and sparingly and by leave of the elders. Nevertheless, matters of doctrine were not to be assailed lest the minister suffer reproach. Again Anne recognized a blow struck at her, and we may believe with difficulty held her speech.

Next they voted that a member of a church could not sever his connection with it on the ground that he disagreed with the minister's theology, unless it was something fundamental. If he asked dismissal to another church, he was to be denied for his own good. This was Blow Number Three, struck at Anne through those friends of hers who had sought dismissal from Pastor Wilson's ministrations.

Her dearest friend struck the shrewdest blow of all, however, for she now heard John Cotton ally himself, in spirit if not in actual deed, with the opposition. The Council had reduced the points of difference between Cotton and Wheelwright on the one hand and the rest of the ministers on the other to three statements. To these three Wheelwright refused to agree, but Cotton at last consented.

At the risk of completely paralyzing a modern reader, repeating the three points in the language in which they put them on record at the time is worthwhile. By this method, we can show how nebulous was the clearest statement that they could reach after three weeks of discussion. Here are the points at issue:

"1. That 'the new creature' is not the person of a believer, but a body of saving graces in such a one; and that Christ, as a head, doth enliven or quicken, preserve or act the same, but Christ himself is no part of this 'new creature.'

2. That though, in effectual calling (in which the answer of the soul is by active faith, wrought at the same instant by the Spirit) justification and sanctification be all together in them; yet God doth not justify a man, before he be effectually called, and so a believer.

3. That Christ and his benefits may be offered and exhibited to a man under a Covenant of Works, but not in or by a Covenant of Works."

Rejecting these, Wheelwright faced exile. Accepting them, Cotton turned his back on an old friend. One can forgive Cotton for saying that he saw them as the other ministers saw them, for anyone could, seemingly, see what he chose in such pronouncements. On the other hand, we can equally understand Wheelwright's stubborn refusal.

Compromise lay in Cotton's nature, obduracy in Wheelwright's.

Anne Hutchinson, listening with sinking heart to the answer of Cotton, realized that here was a virtual recantation. He was no longer her partisan, however sincerely he might remain her friend. Here was a blow at her most vulnerable part, her warm and generous affections.

The conclusion of the Synod was satisfactory to all of the ministers except Wheelwright. Cotton declared that he esteemed some of the eighty-two opinions garnered in for discussion to be blasphemies, some heretical, many of them erroneous, "and almost all of them incommodiously expressed." John Winthrop said that the Synod had been a lovely occasion. He proposed that "seeing the Lord had been so graciously present in this assembly, and matters had been carried on so peaceably and concluded so comfortably in all love, etc., if it were not fit to have the like meeting once a year, or at least the next year, to settle what remained to be settled, or if but to nourish love, etc."

How hopeful to suppose that what remained to be settled could ever be settled!

The rest of the assembly thought Winthrop's idea might be a good one. However, they failed to confirm it by vote.

Later, Winthrop changed his mind about the success

of the Synod. "There was great hope," he wrote, looking back upon it, "that the late general assembly would have had some good effect in pacifying the troubles and dissensions about religion; but it fell out otherwise." Then he puts the blame on the other side. "For though Mr. Wheelwright and those of his party had been clearly confuted and confounded in the assembly, yet they persisted in their opinions, and were as busy nourishing contentions (the principal of them) as before."

Anne Hutchinson, like Wheelwright, was not the kind of person to be changed by confuting and confounding. Bereft of Vane and of Cotton, with Wheelwright's fate sealed except for the actual formality of a vote, she still stood firmly on her convictions, still undismayed. She needed to put her trust in something stable, for she was immediately approaching the great trial of her life. The clerical party, fortified by the outcome of the Synod, was now resolved to get rid of all those who were troubling them.

As soon as the Synod was over, they dissolved the General Court, though it had been elected for a whole year, and called a new election. This was especially an attack at the Boston representatives who were Hutchinson men. Vane had gone home, Hough was dropped, but the three deputies that Boston now chose were still of a Hutchinsonian stripe — Coddington (re-elected), Coggeshall, and Aspinwall. On the second of November the new Court convened. Its first business was to expel Aspinwall on the ground that he was the author of that much-talked-of Petition, first presented in March and renewed at the May election. Coggeshall remonstrated at the treatment of Aspinwall and he, too, was put out. Coddington they did not quite dare to touch.

Again the Boston freemen voted for their representatives to the General Court. This time there was dissension. At Cotton's advice they chose William Colburn and John Oliver, brother of the ruling elder of the Boston church. Of these, they refused Oliver his seat because he, too, had been a signer of the Petition. Boston ignored the order to fill his place and got along with only two representatives.

Now the lines drew closer around Anne Hutchinson. "The General Court, being assembled . . . and finding upon consultation that two so opposite parties could not continue in the same body without apparent hazard of ruin to the whole, agreed to send away some of the principal." One item alone must be disposed of before the Court turned its attention to the lady. That was the matter of John Wheelwright's sentence. He had been convicted of "constructive sedition" the previous March and had been awaiting the sentence, with opportunity to retract, ever since. He had not retracted and the Court had no patience left. Questioned for a night and a day, he tried to do as Vane had advised and appeal to the king. Yet Massachusetts then, as always from the very beginning, showed that it meant to endure no appeal from its courts to the King and refused to let Wheelwright's appeal stand. They declared that they held him responsible for the trouble in the colony and sentenced him to go into exile the following March and in the meantime to keep silent. Refusing to be silenced, he appealed for simple banishment, and the Court gave him two weeks in which to wind up his affairs and be gone.

So Wheelwright must go. Vane had gone. Cotton? Just where was Cotton? Anne did not exactly know, but he was not with her. She admired him as much as ever, but she no longer felt free to consult him. Before this she had accepted him as one of the verities; whatever happened, John Cotton was there. Now the thought of Cotton saddened her. There was an aching core at the center of all her thoughts, and the core was her grieving over Cotton.

Nevertheless, matters pressed so hard that there was no time for brooding. There was nothing for her to do except to go on — alone if need be — yet not alone, for she still had many faithful friends. And William had no word of complaint.

Now the Court, at the very session that had banished Wheelwright, turned its attention immediately upon Anne. That breeder and nourisher of all these distempers! That chief fomenter! The vote of the Court was "that Mistress Anne Hutchinson be summoned for traducing the ministers and their ministry in the country."

She, Anne Hutchinson, the gentlewoman, the leader of Boston society, the friend of Vane — and of Cotton, the head of a party that still dominated the Boston church and had honeycombed the other towns, she, the beloved Lady Bountiful of Boston, was to be brought before the bar of the Court for slander, for a tattling tongue, like any common talemonger!

XIV

THE TRIAL

The scene is set for the trial of Anne Hutchinson. The criminal trial of a woman who had devoted her life to helping the sick and the needy, and to the teaching of God's Word! A woman, alas, who had exercised her right to free judgment and free speech without thought of where it might lead her.

It was in Newtowne, well away from the sympathetic atmosphere of her hometown. The day was one of those brief, cheerless, relentless days of November that bring New England its first taste of winter. The weather that fall of 1637 had been raw and cold. The week before there had been a snowstorm. Already the ice was piling up along the Charles' bank.

The interior of the church where they brought Anne to trial was a single room, small, bare, unlighted and unheated, but probably filled to its entire seating capacity. Below the preacher's desk were some chairs and a table. The rest of the furniture consisted of rough wooden benches. The persons in this drama to be enacted were Governor John Winthrop, seated behind the table, the secretary of the colony beside him, and at the front where the Governor could confer with them, the magistrates. Behind them sat the deputies or representatives, nearly all of the thirty-two returned from the towns of the colony. They were a solid, stern and bitter-looking set of men, hard to move when they had made up their minds.

In front of the table stood an English matron forty-six years old, a gentlewoman of a proud and haughty carriage. She had no counsel, for her trial, after the custom of the colony, was to be a hearing in open legislative session.

Besides these, there were as many spectators as could get into the little room, especially ministers who were there as advisers and witnesses for the colony. Our old friends Shepard, Wilson, Peter, Weld, Symmes, and Phillips were present. Several of these men, back in England, had known what it was to be on trial for differing with the authorities in matters of religion.

Against Anne was the man who was both judge and prosecutor, John Winthrop. Against her was the Deputy-Governor Dudley — always. The other magistrates — Endicott, Bradstreet, Harlakenden, Stoughton, and Nowell — cross-questioned her and witnessed against her. Among the deputies, Coddington was the only one who defended her — to his own injury. Deacon Coggeshall, already disfranchised, and Elder Leverett of Boston were there to witness for her. Shepard, there in his own church, showed his gentler side, and Cotton, as he always did, tried to clear away the difficulties and make all smooth. The other ministers were definitely out for a conviction. The deputies, with three exceptions, were antagonistic.

In addition to the Court scribe there was evidently a partisan in the room taking notes for the prisoner. Anne referred to the day's notes each night and one of the two reports handed down was clearly made by a friendly hand. Both reports agree in substance but differ in wording and atmosphere.

The Governor, patient but anxious to put an end to the troubles of the colony, opened the proceedings with an arraignment:

"You are called here," he said, to the daughter of Francis Marbury, "as one of those who have troubled the peace of the Commonwealth and the churches. You are known to have had a great share in spreading the opinions that are the cause of our trouble, and to be closely related to some whom the Court have taken notice of before. You have said things prejudicial to the honor of the churches and the ministers and you have held meetings at your house that have been condemned by the general assembly.

Though these have been censured as not tolerable or comely, or fitting for your sex, you have kept on. Therefore, we have summoned you so that we may either rescue you and make you a profitable member among us; or, if you be obstinate, take such action that you may trouble us no longer. Therefore I entreat you to say whether you do or do not justify Mr. Wheelwright's sermon and the Petition."

Anne's answer was swift. "I am called here to answer before you, but I hear nothing laid to my charge."

"I have told you already. What more can I do?"

"Name one, I pray you."

"Why, for one thing, you harbored and countenanced those that are parties of this faction that we spoke of."

"That's a matter of conscience, sir."

"You must control your conscience, or it must be controlled for you."

Her eyes flashed. "What law have I transgressed?"

The Governor thereupon explained that she had disobeyed the commandment to honor father and mother because (*a*) she had encouraged those who signed the Petition for Wheelwright, (*b*) the Petition was obnoxious to the magistrates, (*c*) the magistrates were her father and mother in the law; therefore, she had dishonored her father and mother.

"I deny it," she cried. "I am to obey you only in the Lord."

"You have joined them in the faction."

"In what faction have I joined them?"

"In presenting the Petition . . ."

"I did not sign it."

"You have counseled them."

"Wherein?"

"Why — in entertaining them."

"What breach of law is that, sir?"

"Why, dishonoring your parents."

And so the circle ran. Winthrop based his argument on the Westminster Catechism, which defined "father and mother" in the Fifth Commandment as "all superiors in age and gifts, especially those over us in authority," but his argument had an unpleasant Laud-and-High-Commission flavor to those in the company who had heard something like it to their own sorrow in England.

As Anne fenced delightedly with his words, Winthrop lost his temper for a minute. "We do not mean to talk with one of your sex about this," he said brusquely. "You do adhere to them and you do try to promote this faction, and so you do dishonor us."

So much for that. He now tried something else.

"What of your weekly meetings?" he asked.

Here the accused was on even surer ground.

"When I first came to this land," she said, "because I did not go to such meetings, it was presently reported that I did not allow of such meetings, but held them unlawful and did despise all ordinances. Upon that a friend came unto me and told me of it, and I to prevent such aspersions took it up, but it was in practice before I came. Therefore, I was not the first."

She reminded the Judge of the clear rule in Titus, wherein the older women are told to instruct the younger. But Winthrop, too, could be a casuist; he, too, was trained in Biblical argumentation. "Ah," said he, "that means privately and gives no warrant for set meetings like yours. Besides," with a touch of gallantry, "you take it upon yourself to teach many older than yourself. Nor do you teach them 'to keep at home' as the apostle commands."[1] A ghost of a smile flickered over the faces of the Court.

Anne seemed to rise to the bait. "Will it please you to answer this and give me a rule that I may follow? If any come to my house to be instructed in the ways of God, what rule have I to send them away?"

"You must show your rule for receiving them," said the Governor.

"I have."

"I deny it."

"To me it is a rule."

"You must know," the Governor explained, "that there is no rule in the Scripture that contradicts another." Yet when she insisted upon knowing *what* rule kept her from teaching those who asked her instruction, the Governor had to fall back on the arm of the law. "We are your judges," he said, "and not you ours. And we must compel you to it."

"Very well," she said sweetly. "If it please you by authority to put it down, I will freely let you. For I am subject to your authority."

The magistrates interposed at this point to express their opinions about women's meetings. Simon Bradstreet, husband of the first New England lady poet, Anne Dudley Bradstreet, said he was not against all women's meetings. Thomas Dudley, father of the poetess and not so well trained, wanted to know whether there were any men at the meetings. There were two meetings, said the Chair.

"How?" exclaimed Dudley. "Are there two meetings?"

"Ay, sir," said Anne, "I will not equivocate. There is a meeting for men and women and there is a meeting only for women."

"Who teaches in the men's meeting?" inquired John Endicott. "Do not women sometimes?"

"Never as I heard," said the prisoner. "Not one." But,

she supposed that if a man came and asked for light on religious matters she might give it. "Aquila and Priscilla took it upon themselves to instruct Apollos, though he was a man of good parts."

"Priscilla with her husband took Apollos home to instruct him privately. Therefore Mistress Hutchinson, without her husband, may teach sixty or eighty!" The Governor was not above a private dig. Everybody knew William Hutchinson was no teacher!

"I ask them not," she replied calmly. "If they come to me, I may instruct them."

The Governor made as if to speak. However, before he could utter another word, Anne turned white and had to brace herself against the table. She had been standing for two hours while her judges sat at ease.

"May I sit down?" she asked. "I am somewhat weary."

With a bow Governor Winthrop acquiesced. But no shade of sympathy crossed his grave features, or the features of any of the judges. Deep in their hearts they must have felt surprise. Anne had long since proved her physical strength and they held her as capable of endurance as any man. However, now she was pregnant — again.*

So far the contest of wits had been decidedly in Anne's

---

* This was her sixteenth pregnancy.

favor and the Governor's dignity had suffered. Conscious of this and evidently not caring to prolong the battle, Winthrop summed up the case in practically the same words he had used before. Her meetings seduced honest people who attended. The trouble in the colony all came from those who frequented the meetings, "so that now they are flown off from the magistrates and the ministers and this only since they went to her." And that anyway it did not stand well with the Commonwealth that families be neglected with so many neighbors and dames spending their time thus. "There is no rule of God authorizing such meetings. So what hurt comes from it you are responsible for and we who permit it."

Her answer was an unconditional denial. "Sir, I do not believe that to be so," she said flatly.

Could they get nothing from her but stubborn contradiction?

All this was a mere preamble to the real charge. It was Thomas Dudley who, thinking too much time had been spent on minor issues, focussed the attention of the Court upon the real trouble, the long series of dissensions that had torn the colony for the past three years, ever since this lady came to the land.

"Within half a year of her coming," said Dudley, "she had vented divers of her strange opinions and had made parties in the country and at length it comes that Mr. Cotton and Mr. Vane were of her judgment, but Mr. Cotton hath cleared himself that he was not of that mind. But now it doth appear that Mrs. Hutchinson hath forestalled the minds of many by their resort to her meetings, so that now she hath a potent party in the country."

The prosecution then proceeded to the foundation of their charge. They accused Anne of saying publicly that Mr. Cotton alone preached a Covenant of Grace, and that the other ministers preached a Covenant of Works.

"I pray, sir, prove it," Anne said. "Prove that I said they preached nothing but a Covenant of Works."

"Nothing but a Covenant of Works!" growled Dudley. "Why, a Jesuit can preach the truth sometimes!"

"Well, then, when did I say they preached a Covenant of Works?"

"At Mr. Cotton's house," said Hugh Peter, reminding her of the time when they met and asked her about the difference between them and Cotton.

The Marbury temper blazed up. Turning upon her accusers like a tigress at bay, she protested hotly that it was one thing to speak publicly and quite another to speak privately to those who came in a way of friendship.

The ministers who were on hand as witnesses — Peter,

Weld, Symmes, Eliot, Phillips and Shepard — stuck grimly to their testimony. They said that they had heard of the distinction she drew between them and Mr. Cotton. They had met with "this gentlewoman" at the house of Mr. Cotton and had asked her what she meant. She had been "very tender" with them at first, but had finally said it was true, there was a difference between Mr. Cotton's preaching and theirs. She had said they could not preach a Covenant of Grace because they were not sealed by the Spirit and were not able ministers of the New Testament.

"And since then," said Hugh Peter, "we have gone with tears, some of us, to her, to find if she held the same opinion."

"If our pastor, Mr. Wilson, would show his writings," Anne replied to this, "you would see what I said and that many things are not as is reported."

But Mr. Wilson said that he had not the report with him.

Anne was not surprised. She knew Wilson's feelings toward her only too well and she did not expect him to help her out. But she desired to bring before the Court the fact that notes had been taken at that meeting in Mr. Cotton's house and that she was willing to have them read.

Again Anne declared with dignity that her remarks had been private, not public. Nevertheless, she had said merely that they did not preach a Covenant of Grace as Mr. Cotton did, but preached a Covenant of Works as did the Apostles before the Ascension.

Here Dudley, who had taken an active part in the prosecution and was out for Cotton's head, interposed. "I will make it plain," he declared, "that you said they were not able ministers of the New Testament, but Mr. Cotton only."

"If ever I spake that, I proved it by God's Word," replied the defendant.

"Very well, very well," said the Court. There was a little more fencing about the testimony of the ministers. However, in the midst of the wrangle, the early November darkness shut down over the village and Governor Winthrop had to adjourn the meeting.

"The time grows late," he said. "We shall therefore give you a little more time to consider of it. I only add this," he concluded with sarcasm, "that it is well observed that Mrs. Hutchinson can tell when to speak and when to hold her tongue."

If only she had really been able to tell that, her fate would have been different!

Thus ended the first day of the trial, with nothing proved against Anne. The air was full of metaphysical-theological phrases that could be interpreted a hundred ways, and with patent proof that the real basis of the charge against her lay in the injured feelings of the clergy.

The two parties dispersed to their night's quarters to think over what had been said, and to reassemble in the morning, each with new ammunition. Anne had no fear for the outcome.

1. The Colony was a religious organization, and what hurt Anne most was a rule established approximately 1600 years before, by St. Paul (or by later writers/translators/revisers, who changed much in the Scriptures).

These words, found in I Corinthians 14:34-35, are as follows: "Let your women keep silence in the churches: for it is not permitted unto them to speak; but they are commanded to be under obedience, as also saith the law. And if they will learn anything, let them ask their husbands at home: for it is a shame for women to speak in the church."

The tragedy of Anne's life was that she was *born* to be a minister, and with a highly developed inspiration, to counsel and guide others in religious matters. Her husband was only a simple merchant; she could ask him nothing religious. He asked *her*. So, an ancient church rule, still maintained, was used against Anne Hutchinson, to the hurt (and later death) of herself and her offspring. She was a lady born too soon. Or, one might say, this great spirit was born in a body of the wrong gender, for that backward time.

XV

"WE SHALL ALL DIE FASTING!"

Early the next morning the Court put on greatcoats and scarves and convened again in the same place. Anne Hutchinson had stayed awake the night before, reading over the notes of the previous day's meeting which her unnamed friend — no one has yet discovered who it was — had taken for her. She had found a chance for a counterattack. From the notes she discovered "some things not to be as alleged." Therefore, before the Court had really got settled to work, she requested that the ministers, since they were testifying in their own case, be required to take an oath.

That was a bomb! She outraged the clergy and the Court was aghast. It was nothing short of an insult to ask the most revered men in the colony, the spiritual leaders of the country, to give an oath to speak the truth. There followed a debate on this point, which lasted some time. Winthrop was of the opinion that there was no need of an oath since this was not a trial by jury. "Moreover," he added, "we know that what they have said is true and confirmed by divers persons." Endicott declared, "A sign it is what respect she has to the ministers' words!" One Watertown deputy argued that he was afraid of an oath lest God's name be taken in vain: "Suppose the ministers should be mistaken, you will make them sin if you urge them to swear."

Dudley attempted to sidetrack the issue by asking about the witnesses for the defendant: "Mark what a flourish Mrs. Hutchinson puts upon the business that she had witnesses to disprove what was said, and here is no man in court!" This she quietly disposed of by replying, "If you do not call them in, that is nothing to me. An oath is the end of the strife," she insisted, "and it is God's ordinance."

At this, some of the Court advised having the ministers take an oath, inasmuch as it was a case that had aroused so much excitement throughout the colony. A few of them, headed by Hugh Peter, said they were willing to be sworn for the sake of ending the dispute. "We do not desire to be so narrow to the Court and this gentlewoman about times and seasons," was Peter's magnanimous way of putting it. So Governor Winthrop, tired of the delay, required three of the clergymen to go through the form.

"It would be well," drily suggested Coggeshall, the dismissed Boston deputy, there as witness for the defendant, "that the ministers consult with Mr. Cotton and come to an agreement about what they are to say." Coggeshall's sarcasm seemed flippant and out of place to the magistrates. "This carriage of yours," Endicott rapped out, "tends to further casting of dirt upon the face of the judge."

Before the ministers repeated their testimony under oath, they allowed Anne to have her witnesses called. The first was this same Coggeshall, who seems to have become discouraged by the effect of his first attempt to speak. Now, Hugh Peter used his domineering tone to browbeat Coggeshall into silence. Coggeshall began: "I was present at the conference between Mrs. Hutchinson and the ministers, and I dare say that she did not say all that they lay against her . . ."

Peter interrupted him, "How dare you look into the face of the Court and say such a word?"

"Mr. Peter takes it upon himself to forbid me," Coggeshall replied stiffly. "I shall be silent." And silent he was, more is the pity.

No help there, thought Anne.

Her second witness was Elder Leverett of the Boston church. He had been present, he said, at the conference in question. He had heard Mr. Peter vehemently entreat Anne Hutchinson to point out the difference between his preaching and Mr. Cotton's. She had replied that the difference was the same as that between the Apostles before and after the Ascension. That they had not received the seal of the Spirit and therefore, preached with less assurance. So, Mr. Peter and the others, not having the same assurance of God's favor as Mr. Cotton, could not preach a Covenant of Grace as well as he could.

"Don't you remember she said they were not able ministers of the New Testament?" asked the Governor.

Before Leverett could answer, Anne broke in. "Mr. Weld and I talked an hour at the window. If I said it at all, I said it then." She turned to Mr. Weld. "Don't you remember I came to the window when you were writing and then spake to you?"

"No, truly," replied Weld.

"But I do, very well," said Anne.

Not much help for Anne there, either.

Three of the ministers were next sworn, and testified that the accused had said they were not able ministers.

Then they called upon Mr. Cotton to give his account. Anne watched that dear and kindly face, she heard that winning voice that had cleared away so many difficulties. Hope stirred within her, only to be checked by the recollection that Cotton had thrown in his lot with the rest of the clergy. And yet, he could do so much.

Mr. Cotton did his best. He was by nature tolerant. The whole wrangle was distasteful to him and he earnestly wished that it had never been started. If it had been left to him, he could have settled it by tactful arbitration and even now he very nearly accomplished it. Nevertheless, he could not counteract Anne's too-eager tongue.

He made a deft and capable address. He explained terms, smoothed over difficulties, and put a new interpretation on what was said at the conference. So, when he finished there seemed to be little distinction between what the ministers said and what Anne Hutchinson said. The gist of his talk was that the ministers did not take Anne Hutchinson's remarks as hard at the conference as they had since. They also said rumor would less easily stir them up, in the future, and would talk no more about it.

Under the lead of Peter, the ministers questioned Cotton sharply, but they could not shake him. At last Dudley put the interrogation straight: "Did Mrs. Hutchinson say they were not able ministers of the New Testament?"

"I do not remember it," replied the grave, gentle, convincing voice of Cotton.

A wave of relief spread over the portion of the audience that was friendly to Anne. Cotton had deliberately sided with her. To the forefront of the opposition his words were not acceptable. Dudley and Peter, in particular, showed their disapproval. However, with the main body, the bottom of the prosecution had apparently fallen through. It looked as if the Court would have to let her go unless they allowed themselves to convict her on general principles, as they might well have liked to do.

Then came her undoing.

Perhaps it was her feeling of elation over her apparent victory. John Winthrop thought it was no less than God's providence. Whatever may have prompted her, at this point she began to talk. Out of her own mouth, she furnished the ground of her conviction. Probably the cause was a feeling of relief that lifted her out of all common sense. That relief and her incorrigible disposition to teach, impelled her to proclaim her experience with the enthusiasm that her judges hated.

Thus run the records:

"Upon this she began to speak her mind, and to tell of the manner of God's dealing with her, and how He had revealed Himself to her, and made her know what she had to do. The Governor perceiving whereabout she went, interrupted her and would have kept her to the matter in hand, but seeing her very unwilling to be taken of, he permitted her to proceed."

So she told of her life in Old England, of her troubles

about forms of worship and her temptation to turn Separatist. She spoke of her day of fasting and prayer, and her sure guidance out of God's Word. "And upon this it was revealed to me that the ministers of England were Antichrists. But I knew not how to bear this; I did in my heart rise up against it."

Still, she struggled for a twelvemonth with her problem. At last she saw the light and it was revealed to her which was the voice of Moses, which of John the Baptist, and which of Christ. "The voice of my Beloved I have distinguished from the voice of strangers. Henceforth I have been more choice whom I heard, for after our teacher Mr. Cotton and my brother Wheelwright were put down, there was none in England that I durst hear. Then it pleased God to reveal himself to me in that Scripture of Isaiah (30:20): 'and though the Lord give you the bread of adversity, and the water of affliction, yet shall not thy teachers be removed into a corner anymore, but thine eyes shall see thy teachers.'

"Then did the Lord reveal himself to me, sitting upon a Throne of Justice, and all the world appearing before Him, and, though I must come to New England, yet I must not fear nor be dismayed. And I could not be at rest but I must come hither. The Lord brought another Scripture to me: 'For the Lord spake thus to me with a strong hand

and instructed me that I should not walk in the way of this people!'" (Isaiah 8:11)

Again, it was revealed to her that plots should be made against her, but He that delivered Daniel and the children of Israel, His hand was not shortened.

"And behold! This Scripture is fulfilled this day in my eyes. Therefore, take heed what you go about to do unto me. You have power over my body, but the Lord Jesus hath power over my body and soul; neither can you do me any harm.

"I fear none but the great Jehovah, which hath foretold me of these things, and I do verily believe that He will deliver me out of your hands. Therefore, take heed how you proceed against me, for I know that for this you go about to do to me, you will bring a curse upon you and your posterity, and the mouth of the Lord hath spoken it."

Exhausted, she paused.

"How do you know it was God that did reveal these things and not Satan?" demanded Magistrate Nowell.

"How did Abraham know that it was God that did bid him offer his son?" she returned.

"By an immediate voice," explained Dudley.

"So to me by an immediate revelation," the amazing woman calmly continued.

"An immediate revelation!"

"By the voice of His own Spirit to my soul," she declared.

"I may read Scripture," said Harlakenden, another magistrate, "and the most glorious hypocrite may read it and yet go down to hell."

"It may be so," she said, unshaken.

Deluded woman, she no doubt thought that she had already been delivered. However, in the moment of victory, defeat had come upon her. Her utterances were wholly antagonistic to the minds of her listeners. If Harry Vane had been there, he would have been experimentalist enough to see possible truth in her assertions. However, to men like Endicott and Dudley, Peter and Weld, to Winthrop, even to Cotton, she had touched on the cardinal evil that besets free religion — that is, the belief that God's inspiration is transmitted directly to human beings. These men trusted in God's providences. They thought they saw them manifested in the most trifling circumstances. They were always seeing the hand of God in the weather, in the action of animals, in nature's workings. No one could have been more superstitious than they. Nevertheless, they drew a strict line between such outward warnings of God's will and any message transmitted by Him directly to the heart and mind of a believer. They simply would not have it. God's Word was in the Scriptures. He had set it all down there. It was at hand for one's study. It was all there and He was never going to add anything to it, either in the writings or utterances of His saints or in the meditations of their hearts. Revelation was *finished*. All that was left for men was to study and interpret His revelations as given in His Word. But this woman!

The storm broke upon her. Even Cotton could not help her. He did not agree with her and, for once, he was powerless to make the difference between her views and theirs dissolve into thin air. Mr. Bartholomew remembered that she had talked about having revelations on the way to New England.

"I say the same thing again," she persisted.

"Does her reverend teacher," cried Endicott, "does he condescend to such revelations as have here been spoken of?"

Cotton did his best to draw a distinction between revelations that were fantastical and led to danger and those that came spontaneously to a prayerful and worshipful spirit. As for Anne Hutchinson's being delivered by God's providence, he did not accept present-day miracles. He looked upon miracles and "revelations without the Word" as delusions. "And I think so doth she, too, as I understand her," he added kindly.

Endicott was not satisfied. "Do you witness for her

or against her?" he demanded. "I am tender of you, sir, and there lies much upon you in this particular, for the answer of Mr. Cotton does not free him from that way which his last answer did bring upon him."

Cotton's answer satisfied Endicott. But not Dudley! Dudley set his jaw stiffly and said he was not content. He could not endure hearing Mr. Cotton make excuses for his favorite parishioner, and he said bluntly, "Sir, you weary me and you do not satisfy me."

This was perhaps the most dangerous moment that Cotton had ever faced. Nevertheless, for Anne there was the sweet comfort of feeling that he was at least trying to help her. Many of the ministers and magistrates set upon Cotton until Winthrop came to the rescue, saying that they were not there to try Mr. Cotton, but the party standing here before them.

By this time proceedings had grown entirely unparliamentary and Winthrop does not seem to have attempted to keep order. Magistrates, clergy, and deputies all talked at once. Winthrop himself began to see "a marvellous providence of God — to bring things to this pass that they are."

"We have been hearkening about the trial of this thing," he said, "and now the mercy of God by a providence hath answered our desires and led her to lay open herself and the ground of all these disturbances to be by revelations . . ." It is hard to see the difference between Winthrop's use of the word "providence" and hers. Nevertheless, the difference was clear enough in his mind. ". . . I would that those were cut off that trouble us, for this is the thing that hath been the root of all mischief — Aye! It is the most desperate enthusiasm in the world, for nothing but a word comes to her mind and then an application is made which is nothing to the purpose, and this is her revelations!"

The scorn with which he spoke! She provoked him out of all patience, a reasonable man driven beyond endurance. Enthusiasms! Revelations! The last wile of Satan!

"A devilish delusion!" said Magistrate Nowell.

"I never saw such revelations as these even among the enthusiasts and Anabaptists," echoed Dudley. Then, with a dig at Cotton, "I am sorry Mr. Cotton stands up for her."

"Very disputable that which our brother Cotton hath spoken," insisted Peter, in whom professional jealously had long rankled. "I profess I thought Mr. Cotton would never have taken her part."

Everyone put in his word about revelations. They grounded all those disturbances among the Germans on revelations — taking arms against the government and cutting one another's throats. The devil was in it, and the devil deluded Anne Hutchinson. Bartholomew of Ipswich added that his wife had told him that Mr. Wheelwright was not acquainted with this way until Anne Hutchinson imparted it to him. Brown of Watertown said he thought she deserved all the censure she had received and more too, "for all those bastardly errors of the Synod have come out of this cursed fountain."

On the tide of their strong language Winthrop was about to put the question, when Coddington, who had kept silent before, rose and asked for a hearing. His dignity and reputation caused a hush.

"Suppose," he asked, "if Mrs. Hutchinson had held the meetings at her house just for her own family, could not others have attended?"

"If you have nothing else to say, Mr. Coddington, it is a pity you should interrupt us," answered Winthrop.

Yet Coddington, who had both influence and energy, refused to be put off. He went on to say that the same man ought not to be judge and accuser in the same case. He said that they had proved nothing against Anne Hutchinson except that she had said the other ministers did not preach a Covenant of Grace as clearly as Cotton did, and that they were in the state of the Apostles before the Ascension, which was no disparagement.

"But her own words just now are ground for conviction," urged Winthrop.

"Words uttered in uplifted moments are not deserving of extreme punishment. I do beseech you," pleaded Coddington, "do not speak so as to force things along, for I for my part do not see any equity in your proceedings. Here is no law of God that she hath broken, neither any law of the country."

His speech created some division of opinion. There was a great whispering among the Court members, one saying one thing and one another, while Anne turned a weary but thankful glance upon her defender. Even at this late moment, Coddington might have been of some avail had not Deputy-Governor Dudley been hungry.

"We shall all die fasting!" Dudley cried — and the Court agreed.

After a little more demur on the part of one or two, Winthrop in his capacity as moderator of the Court put the question. As judge, he formulated the question and then instructed them how to vote.

"The Court hath already declared themselves satisfied concerning the things you hear, and concerning the troublesomeness of her spirit, and the danger of her course amongst us, which is not to be suffered. Therefore, if it is the mind of the Court that Mrs. Hutchinson for these things that appear before us, is unfit for our society — and if it be the mind of the Court that she shall be banished out of our liberties, and imprisoned until she be sent away, let them hold up their hands."

All but three held up their hands. Two voted no, Coddington and Colburn of Boston. William Jennison of Watertown said he could not vote either way.

"Mrs. Hutchinson," said the Governor, "you hear the sentence of the Court. It is that you are banished from out our jurisdiction as being a woman not fit for our society. And you are to be imprisoned till the Court send you away."

"I desire to know," demanded the still undefeated woman, "wherefore I am banished."

"Say no more," was the stern and weary rejoinder.

"The Court knows wherefore and is satisfied." He might have said, "Because we are all hungry and want to go home."

So the sentence is set down in the Colony Records of Massachusetts:

"Mrs. Hutchinson, (the wife of Mr. William Hutchinson) being convented for traducing the ministers and their ministry in the country, she declared voluntarily her revelations for her ground and that she should be delivered and the Court ruined, with their posterity;

thereupon was banished, and in the meantime was committed to Mr. Joseph Weld of Roxbury until the Court shall dispose of her."

The clergy had won a victory.

The Court, exhausted, took a recess. John Winthrop went home to face his gentle wife. Anne Hutchinson was conveyed away from her friends to Roxbury. She truly believed that God would save her from calamity.

"Now, having seen Him Who is invisible," she had told the Court, "I fear not what man can do unto me."

XVI

THE WINTER AT ROXBURY

There was only one man in the colony who could possibly have saved Anne Hutchinson from banishment after she began to talk about her revelations. That was John Winthrop. William Coddington, a man of means and former treasurer of the colony, did not avail. John Cotton, the beloved and reverend teacher, did not avail in spite of his honest effort. If she had not broached her revelations, he might have averted the sentence. However, he could not control her too ingenuous and willing tongue. Even if Winthrop, too, had wanted to save her and had so directed the meeting at this time, she would likely enough have been punished sooner or later. Because, sooner or later, she would have talked to her own hurt. She could not have forborne it. Quite naturally she would have looked upon her escape as a vindication. She would have pushed her activities all the more eagerly, and the ministers would not have forgotten her criticism.

In any case, Winthrop did not want her in the colony any longer. He was tired of the conflict that marked her presence. He cared more about the peace of the colony than he did about the fine distinctions between a Covenant of Works and a Covenant of Grace, a great seal and a little seal, and the presence of the Holy Ghost in a believer. "Troubling the colony" was the cardinal sin in his eyes. At Wheelwright's trial Winthrop constantly referred to "cause of disturbance," "alienated minds" and "the troubling of our peace." All that troubled them should go, especially Anne Hutchinson, "chief fomentor and head of troubles."

Winthrop was not quibbling when he seized upon her claim of revelations as grounds for expulsion. He firmly believed that persons who pretended to be inspired were preaching a false and destructive doctrine. His stomach turned against it. It was enthusiasm, little short of insanity. He prided himself upon being a sane and sober man. Revelations! Faugh! What a swarm of noisy, cutthroat, licentious, half naked sectaries* it called to his mind. So he let the meeting have its head and sentence her to banishment. It is interesting to recall that it was the same session of the General Court that ordered the building at Newtowne of the college founded by the colony the year before. So they suckled "Veritas" and intolerance at the

---

* Sectary: a dissenter from an established church, especially a Protestant nonconformist.

same breast.

John Wheelwright's sentence of banishment imposed November 4 was to go into effect in two weeks. Accordingly, he preached a farewell sermon to his Wollaston flock. He said good-bye to his family, to his sister-in-law in her Roxbury seclusion, and to the Hutchinson connection in general. In the New England winter, he started out to find a new home.

That winter, beyond the Merrimac, the snow lay a yard deep from November to March. Wheelwright went to the English settlement on the Piscataqua in what is now New Hampshire. His family, including Grandma Hutchinson, joined him in the spring when he helped to found the settlement at Exeter. Some of the Marbury kindred from England were also members of the Exeter group. Massachusetts was petty enough to write to the Piscataqua people rebuking them for giving aid to one whom Massachusetts had expelled.

After this, Wheelwright lived a long and seemingly happy life, in spite of a succession of lawsuits. After leaving Exeter, he was the pastor of the church at Wells, at Hampton, and later at Salisbury. They say that he returned to England for a time and was entertained by Oliver Cromwell and Sir Harry Vane. Back in the colonies again, he made his peace with Massachusetts. When he died, he was the oldest minister in New England.

After their two tasks of banishing Wheelwright and Anne Hutchinson, the Court took a week's rest. Then they convened again to finish, with fresh zeal, the good work they had begun. They dealt with the halberdiers who had refused to attend Governor Winthrop when he was elected in place of Vane. These, William Baulston and Anne's brother-in-law Edward Hutchinson, who had both signed the famous Boston Petition, were disfranchised and fined respectively twenty and forty pounds. Baulston defiantly said that nowhere else in the world would signers of such a petition have been so treated. Edward Hutchinson said that if the Court fined him it would have to support his family. So, they put him in the jail and after taking a night to think it over, said he was sorry and was released. Later on, the fines of both men were remitted on condition that they leave the colony.

Then came more cleaning up. They called the signers of the Boston Petition before the Court and obliged them to choose between withdrawing their names or being punished. Ten recanted; five or six were disfranchised. They ordered fifty-eight Boston men and seventeen from other towns to give up their arms within ten days. Thus only did the Court feel safe from some riot or "suddaine irruption." That the authorities were in real fear of an uprising in Boston is evidenced by the order that they should transfer the powder and arms belonging to the colony from Boston to Roxbury and Cambridge.

The Colony Records (volume I, pages 207-08) read:

"Whereas the opinions and revelations of Mr. Wheelwright and Mrs. Hutchinson have seduced and led into dangerous errours many of the people heare in New England, insomuch as there is just cause of suspition that they, as others in Germany in former times, may upon some revelation, make some suddaine irruption upon those that differ from them in judgment: for pervention whereof, it is ordered, that all those whose names are underwritten shall (upon warning given or left at their dwelling houses) before the 30th day of November, deliver at Mr. Cane's house at Boston all such guns, pistols, swords, powder, shot and match as they shall bee owners of, or have in their custody, upon paine of ten pounds for every default to bee made thereof; which armes are to bee kept by Mr. Cane till this court shall take further order therein. Also it is ordered upon like penalty of ten pounds, that no man, who is to render his armes by this order, shall buy or borrow any guns, swords, pistols, powder, shot or match, until this court shall take further order therein."

Then follow the names of the culprits.

Among them was that amusing old scamp, Captain

John Underhill. Underhill protested that all states allowed military men more liberty of speech than they did to other men. In the Low Countries he had sometimes spoken quite as freely to Count Nassau. His protest did him no good. He had to suffer with the rest of the signers, who constituted most of the leading members of the Boston church.

There is preserved a courteous letter written by John Winthrop to his erstwhile friends, Coddington, Coggeshall, and Colburn. His letter entreats them to admit their error in signing the Petition and receive the clemency of the Court. In spite of his persuasions, they did not recant. On the contrary, they and the others would have called Governor Winthrop before the church to answer for what he had done as a magistrate. However, he got ahead of them and made a long speech in church. He said, quite truly, that the church had no right to call a magistrate to account for what he did in his official capacity.

In the meantime, while they were arraigning and penalizing her relatives and friends, Anne was spending the winter away from Boston. She was under watch and ward in the house of the wealthiest merchant in the colony, Joseph Weld of Roxbury. "The towne of Roxbury is required to take order for the safe custody of Mrs. Hutchinson," say the Colony Records, "and if any charge arises to be defrayed by her husband." Her own friends and the elders could go to see her, but no one else. Across the road lived the Reverend Thomas Weld, Joseph's brother and one of Anne's dearest foes. She now had the full benefit of his discourse, for he came in to see her almost every day and to labor with her concerning her heresies.

For a time after her sentence, her proud spirit suffered. She was separated from her husband and her children. That winter of 1638 was a bitter, dreary one of more than usual severity, but all the winters seemed severe to those who remembered England. During the long hard months, Anne pondered where she could go when spring came and her banishment should be carried into effect. The miracle that she had so confidently proclaimed perhaps was not going to avert her exile, though it would surely convert it into a blessing. She had torn her patient husband from his comfortable home in England. Now, just when he had taken root again, she had made it necessary for him to find a new home farther on. If possible — was it possible? — they must make some provision for a safe journey. By early summer the time would be accomplished when she must again give birth. If all else failed, she might go north in the spring with Mary Wheelwright.

Or William might succeed in finding a place of shelter somewhere else in the wilderness.

Wherever she might go, the work that she had done in Boston was broken off. Those warm friends that she had bound to herself — by her ministrations and her gifts — must be left behind, or they too must go into exile. Some of them would go. Many would not, could not. Her affections, her pride, her keen sense of responsibility, all were torn and humiliated.

Her adversaries, the ministers, furnished a diversion. Not Mr. Weld alone came constantly to reason with her. The other ministers also "resorted to her many times, laboring to convince her, but in vain; yet they resorted to her still, to the end they might either reclaim her from her errors, or that they might bear witness against them if occasion were." Shepard and Eliot toiled over her with particular zeal, Shepard at least out of charity. Yet not in perfect charity.

It is painful to think of those worthy clergymen coming day after day to badger with their arguments and probe with their questions this one sick, sequestered woman. However, it did her good. She began to thrive on it and it may, conceivably, have saved her reason during those winter months. It supplied her with the ever-welcome recreation of formulating statements and arraying arguments to combat those skilled theologians.

Mr. Weld saw to it that his own church took the lead

in casting out its unclean. Immediately after Anne Hutchinson's conviction, "The church at Roxbury," says Winthrop, "dealt with divers of their members (who had their hands to the petition) and spent many days in public meeting to have brought them to see their sin in that, as also in corrupt opinions, which they held, but could not prevail with them. So they proceeded to two or three admonitions, and, when all was in vain, they cast them out of the church. In their dealing with them, they took some of them in plain lies and other foul distempers." In all the accounts of the Antinomians one of the most frequent complaints was that they lied. Their "lies" seem to have consisted in denying the charges made against them.

Anne's quick wit, her facility with the Scriptures, and her ready tongue enraged her antagonists all the more. In Winthrop's *Short Story of the Rise, Reign and Ruin of the Antinomians* we read: "Mistris Hutchinson, being banished and confined . . . she thought it needlesse to conceale herselfe any longer, neither would Satan lose the opportunity of making choyce of so fit an instrument. . . . Therefore she began now to discover all her mind to such as came to her, so that her opinions came abroad and began to take place among her old disciples, . . . and following the sent from one to another, the root of all was found to be in Mistris Hutchinson; — whereupon they resorted to her many times, labouring to convince her but in vaine."

Her keenest hurt came from the conviction that she had completely lost the support of Cotton.

"And so many of Boston were tainted with them (the errors) as Mr. Cotton, finding how he had been abused, and made (as he himself said) their stalking horse* (for they pretended to hold nothing but what Mr. Cotton held, and himself did think the same), did spend most of his time both publickly and privately, to discover those errours, and to reduce such as were gone astray." Winthrop's picture of Cotton is not an edifying one, that of the benign teacher of the church going about the town, night and day, ferreting out errors in order to clear himself. Certainly Cotton had been closely involved in the so-called Antinomian beliefs. In his *Way of the Congregational Churches Cleared,* he admits as much. He confesses his "wanderings into the horrible errours of the Antinomians and Familists, with his dear friend Mrs. Hutchinson, so far that he came to a resolution to side with her and to

---

* Stalking horse: anything used to disguise or conceal intentions, schemes, or activities.

separate from all the churches in New England as legall Synagogues."

The immediate cause for his withdrawal from his old friend was that matter of revelations or direct inspiration. Like Anne, Cotton was inclined to be a mystic, but not to such an extreme. He held many of her opinions in theory but was repelled by them when he saw them leading into extravagant practice. It is one thing to hold a theory speculatively and quite another to put it into vehement words and deeds. For this reason, he tried to convince Anne and her flock of their errors, and of the injury they had done him in fathering them upon him. Edward Johnson in the *Wonder-Working Providence* delicately expresses Cotton's sentiments: "When they brought their bastardly brat to him they put another vizard* on the face of it."

The Hutchinsonians still persisted in reckoning him as one of their number. When her enemies would taunt Anne with the loss of Cotton, she kept on replying calmly, "No matter what you hear him say in public, we know what he saith to us in private." Nevertheless, to herself, she had to admit that she had lost him.

Roger Williams wrote bitterly of Cotton's "fig-leaf

---

* Vizard: a mask.

255

evasions and distinctions," but there is something to be said for Cotton. He was naturally a man of moderation and averse to exuberance. Being made the spokesman of opinions that took on such guises that he revolted against them was distasteful to him. He cannot be blamed for failing to recognize the children of his own brain after they had been stepfathered so zealously by the more fiercely partisan of Anne's faction.

We may be sure that Thomas Weld and Hugh Peter and some of the other clergymen did not fail to inform Anne Hutchinson that her beloved guide had denied her. Through this woman, they had suffered much in their dignity by being unfavorably compared with Cotton. They would have been more than human if they had not been glad to see the minister who alone, with the exception of Wheelwright, had been under a Covenant of Grace now acknowledging a Covenant of Works.

The theological discussions that the visiting clergymen held with Anne could not be expected to end in reconciliation or in the submission of a woman like her. Instead of changing her mind, they only made her hold her opinions more tenaciously than before. Since her adversaries could not persuade her, they would turn their visits to another purpose. They began to busy themselves with collecting and classifying her so-called errors. In this they had a distinct objective. In March, after having assembled about thirty "errors," they put them to the use for which they had been gleaned.

XVII

THE INQUISITION

Sharpening her wits upon those of her ministerial visitors, Anne counted each forensic victory, retrieved her spirits as the winter advanced and did not foresee the next blow. This was nothing less than excommunication, the last humiliation that could come to her.

The ministers found that they could not make her acknowledge her errors and that she discovered fresh arguments at each of their visits. They also believed that her opinions were still alive in the Boston church. Therefore, they decided that it was not enough simply to send her out of the colony. They were exasperated by the arguments that they had waged with such small success, and wrought up by continually dwelling upon the matter. They could endure it no longer. Consequently, they first conferred with the magistrates and then wrote them a formal letter. In case the Boston church consented to question her, they promised to supply evidence of her heresy. We see the initiative in this further attack upon her, therefore, to have come from the clergy of the colony.

A full report of Anne Hutchinson's excommunication has been found in the papers of Ezra Stiles, at one time President of Yale. Dr. Stiles says that the original manuscript from which he made his copy was inscribed, "Robert Keayne in New England, his Booke, Anno 1638."

At the end of the winter they arranged that she should come before the church after the Thursday lecture, on March 15. They called the meeting two hours earlier than common, at ten in the morning. The Court was then in session in Newtowne, but the Governor and the Treasurer, who were members of the Boston church, were excused from Court in order to attend. It was an opportune time for Anne's opponents. Several of the Boston members, under the leadership of Coddington, had gone away to the south to hunt new homes for themselves. Among them was William Hutchinson. In Winthrop's opinion it was by the good Providence of God that these men were away.

It was a horrifying shock to Anne to be summoned to appear before the church, yet at first she did not sense her full danger. Although sentenced to banishment, she believed that her own town and her own church still sympathized with her. She had had repeated proofs of their devotion. When she had gone into captivity in the fall, she had gone accompanied by the groans and tears of hosts of friends.

On the morning when she was to stand before the church for judgment, she wisely waited until the opening exercises had been finished before she appeared. Then, pale and delicate, she entered the church and walked down to the place appointed for her.

She found the church crowded with its own members, with townsfolk, and visitors from other places. It was the most sensational event of the season, surpassing even the trial of the previous November. No one stayed away who could get to the church and gain admittance. Hard benches and hunger, fatigue and cold, were of no account compared with the thrilling suspense of attending the inquisition. Many in the audience were in sympathy with the accused, had received her benefactions, listened to her teachings, accepted her guidance. But they were not the strongest of her flock. These were themselves under the displeasure of the Court and several of them, as had been noted above, were off hunting for new homes. She missed Coddington and Aspinwall; she missed her good William.

She missed Harry Vane, too. As for John Cotton, she knew too sadly that he was no longer on her side.

After the culprit arrived, they called the church members together to the front seats and one of the elders rose and read the indictment. One by one reverberated the errors discovered by Messrs. Weld, Eliot, Shepard, and others during their winter's sessions. The ministers who were willing to testify had put their names opposite the respective counts for which they had consented to witness.

Anne's first words voiced her natural resentment at the use that had been made of her private conversation. Indignantly she demanded, "What rule in Holy Writ makes it right for the elders of the church to question one in my confinement, pretending they sought light, but seeking to entrap me in mine own words?"

There was no answer and the reading went on.

Whatever modern minds may think of the errors listed, they were of the most tremendous importance in the minds of the clergy of 1638 and of Anne Hutchinson. One was that "the souls of all men (in regard to generation) are mortall like the beasts." On this point, Anne quoted much Scripture and so did the elders. Finally, the Reverend John Davenport of New Haven, who was visiting in Boston, explained that there was a difference between the soul and the spirit. Whereupon Anne said she did see a difference and acknowledged this error. Winthrop observes that it was pride that forbade her giving in to any of the Massachusetts clergy, but let her accept the explanation of Mr. Davenport, who was a stranger. Perhaps Winthrop was right. Anne often showed a proud spirit.

By night they had got through only four of the articles in the indictment and the audience was well-nigh exhausted. They had not been able to get her to concede any point except that one on which Mr. Davenport had shed light. Avalanches of scriptural references had been let loose on both sides, more on theirs than on hers simply because they had more tongues with which to speak. She had lost her temper at Mr. Wilson. She called him to account for what he had said at her trial before the Court, and he, to use Palfrey's expression, had caught the contagion of her anger. Radicals have, from time immemorial, assumed an air of superiority, of commiseration toward those so unfortunate as not to be able to see the new light. This attitude gets under the skin of their opponents and does much to prevent an understanding between the two parties. Anne took that attitude now with the ministers, just as she had taken it constantly in her private conversations with them. It angered them, and this time they had the upper hand.

One of her inquisitors, the Reverend Peter Bulkley of Concord, viewed with alarm Anne Hutchinson's Familistic ideas on marriage. "I desire to know," he asked her, "whether you hold that foul, filthy, and abominable doctrine held by Familists, that of community of women?"

"I hold it not," she answered in quick aversion.

Davenport, who had made her see light on the first of her errors, thought the Concord clergyman's question was based on a right principle. "For," he explained, "if the resurrection be past, then marriage is past." His argument seemed to be something like this: that if the resurrection was nothing but the Christian's union with Christ, as she had said, then all that are united are the children of the resurrection, and therefore are neither to marry nor to give in marriage, and so by consequence all women will be common property. Is it clear? The distinguished theologian from Connecticut seemed to think that it was.

Turgid as the explanation seems to the unversed modern, it was sufficiently lucid to make Anne recoil in horror. "If that is the conclusion to be drawn, I must renounce it, for I abhor that practice," the offended gentlewoman cried.

Night drew on.

While they were mired fast in the fourth article and the company almost frozen and starved, but the culprit still going strong — in spite of the bodily infirmity which Winthrop unchivalrously says was a pretense — the elders decided to push matters along by having her formally admonished. Perhaps an admonition delivered by her once-trusted teacher, John Cotton, might make her acknowledge her errors.

In the congregation were some of Anne's dearest and nearest. Her sons Edward, Richard, and Francis were members of the church, her son-in-law Thomas Savage, and her daughters Faith Savage and Bridget. One of her sons — the report simply says "Mr." Hutchinson — now asked for parliamentary advice on how to express his assent or dissent. Savage made a yet longer and more spirited speech. They had not accused his mother-in-law of any heinous act but only of holding opinions, about which she desired further information. Therefore, he could not vote to have the church proceed yet to admonish her.

Thomas Oliver, the elder, quelled both these young men. He said that it was grief to his spirit, "to see these two brethren talk so much and scruple the proceedings of the church." Therefore, since it was fitting that the vote be unanimous, he moved that these two brethren also be laid under an admonition with their mother, so that the church might proceed without further opposition.

This motion commended itself to Pastor Wilson. They put it, and the whole church by their silence consented. (It seems to have been the custom for only those who were contrary-minded to vote, either by show of hands or by voice. Silence gave consent.)

Thereupon Cotton proceeded to admonish his former

disciple.

He addressed his first words to the young men whose admonition had been left to his discretion. He evidently thought it needful to rebuke them all, root and branch. He began, "You that are her sons and son-in-law," thus including more than the two who had spoken in her defense. He bore heavily upon them, referring to their viperish acts "in eating through the very bowells of their mother, to her ruin, if God do not graciously prevent." "Bowells" seem to have been a favorite part of John Cotton's soul-anatomy, as they were of other theologians of the time. He referred to them twice in the admonition, "with much zeal and detestation of her errours and pride of spirit."

The Keayne-Stiles report of the admonition continues:

"To her first he remembered her of the good way she was in at her first coming, in helping to discover to divers the false bottom they stood upon in trusting to legal works without Christ; then he showed her how, by falling into these groce and fundamentall errours, she had lost the honor of her former service, and done more wrong to Christ and his church than formerly she had done good, and so laid sin to her conscience. He admonished her also of the height of spirit, and charged her solemnly before God and his angels, and churches there assembled, to return from the errours of her ways."

Then he clearly outlined the whole duty of a woman. "The Lord hath endued you with good parts and gifts fit to instruct your children and servants and to be helpful to your husband in the government of the family. God hath bestowed upon you a sharp apprehension, a ready utterance, and ability to express yourself in the cause of God."

From this compliment, he proceeded to the unkindest cut of all. Coming from John Cotton who had been such a trusted friend of her family, the reference to the point brought out by the ingenious Mr. Bulkley and emphasized by Mr. Davenport was hard to bear.

"If the resurrection be past," solemnly averred Mr. Cotton, "then you cannot evade the argument that was pressed upon you by our brother Bulkley and others, that filthy sin of the community of women, and all promiscuous and filthy coming together of men and women, without distinction or relation of marriage, will necessarily follow."

This was his logic. If there be no resurrection of the body, then there is no marriage, he says, and hence women will be held in common use!

Then Cotton reached the climax of contumely: "And, although I have not heard, neither do I think, you have been unfaithful to your husband in his marriage covenant, yet that will follow upon it."

Thus the most honored minister of the church in New England spoke to his parishioner and friend, a gentle-woman on the farther side of forty-five, dignified by her long years of wifehood and motherhood, and patently soon to become again a mother. The gentle John Cotton!

Anne, amazed, recovered herself to make one more protest, apologizing for interrupting Mr. Cotton's admonition. "I would beg forbearance by reason of my weakness, for I fear I shall not remember what I have to say when you are done. All I would say is this, that I did not hold any of these things before my imprisonment."

All the more convinced that she was not speaking the truth, Cotton went on: "I have feared the height of your spirit and being puffed up with your own parts. I charge you to remember the great hurt you have done the churches, the great dishonor you have brought upon Jesus Christ, the evil you have done many a poor soul. Be jealous of your own spirit and take heed how you leaven the hearts of young women with such dangerous principles, and labor to recover them out of the snares which you have drawn them into, and so the Lord carry home to your soul what I have spoken to you in His name."

Realizing that this was in large measure a feministic

movement, Cotton then turned to the sisters of the church and warned them "to take heed of her opinions, and to withhold all countenance and respect from her, lest they should harden her in sin." The women whom she had nursed in travail, to whom she had been counselor, comforter, and benefactor were to return her lovingkindness by "withholding all countenance from her"!

"So she was dismissed and appointed to appear again that day seven-night."

That was all that day, except that Mr. Shepard, formerly inclined to be her friend but now forgetting to be charitable, jumped up as soon as Cotton sat down. He protested her statement that she had not held these errors previous to her Roxbury imprisonment. "I am astonished," he said, "that she should so impudently affirm so horrible an untruth and falsehood in the midst of such a solemn ordinance of Jesus Christ and before such an assembly."

It seemed so easy to say, "You lie!"

The assembly had lasted until eight at night, and according to John Winthrop, "all did acknowledge the special presence of God's spirit therein."

It is hard to believe that the women who had been warned to keep away from their friend Anne Hutchinson felt God's spirit in the warning. If they remembered the lessons of love that she had taught them, it would be very difficult to believe. However, they were all exhausted with the ten-hour session, held without recess for food. They rose stiffly from the hard benches where they had sat so many hours, sick at heart. They were outraged but too tired to protest. They followed their respective lords and masters to the bleak little houses where some of those so clearly defined duties, the government of their families and helpfulness toward their husbands, still awaited them.

Their friend had sunk faint and overspent to her seat. Her sons and her son-in-law, passing out, dared to pay their respects to her. Her daughters had gone forth in tears.

Instead of returning to Roxbury, Anne was to stay with the Cottons. The heads of the church had planned this for her own good. They imagined that they perceived in her quietness and dejection some signs of yielding. Though she were plucked as a brand from the burning, it was better to pluck her — even at the risk of getting a little singed. It sounds like Cotton's suggestion that he and his wife Sarah take her to their home. He had a last hope of saving her soul from destruction, though he could not save her body from exile. Mr. Davenport, too, was staying with him. The learned preacher from New Haven had been so successful in making Anne Hutchinson see light on one disputed point. Therefore, if he had longer opportunity, he might bring her to a better understanding of other points.

Under the forty-pound bond of Edward Hutchinson, Jr., Anne was therefore to be lodged in the house of John Cotton.

So Anne rose — silently for once — and followed her teacher from the church. I hope Sarah Cotton waited for her at the church door. Sarah could not have failed to hear her husband warn the women of the congregation to withhold their countenances from their erring sister. Yet not even that, I believe, could have kept her from drawing Anne's arm within her own and guiding her weary steps along the lane that led from the church to the Cotton house on the easterly slope of Beacon Hill. Cotton and Davenport would walk ahead, deep in talk, and the women would follow. As they passed Anne's own house, let us hope, too, that a group of young people were waiting there, to cling to her and kiss her before she had to go on. If they did, Sarah Cotton would not be the woman to hold it against them or call it a viperish act that would eat through the very bowels of their mother.

Wearily and with fainting spirits, Anne passed to the house of him who had been her guide and her friend, her dear teacher on whose very account she had left England. There, during the week that followed, she was buffeted by the arguments of the two ministers, Cotton and Davenport.

Worn out at last, she gave in. She acknowledged that she had been in the wrong. Her father Francis Marbury had somehow made his peace with the Court of High Commission before he received his London church. So, his daughter now sought to make her peace with the self-constituted High Commission of New England. With the help of Cotton and Davenport, she prepared a paper of recantation. At the next Thursday meeting, when they had ordered that she appear again before the church, it would be read.

Cotton congratulated himself that he had at last accomplished something in her behalf. He could not prevent her exile. Yet perhaps he could avert her excommunication, which to him and to her seemed a far graver calamity. Exile touched only the bodily comfort and temporal prosperity. Excommunication meant a severance with the instruments of God's grace. It meant damnation, unless true repentance was publicly expressed.

Even before Anne's recantation was made public, during the week between her admonition and her second appearance before the church, there were other retractions. Several of her adherents, "divers of our chief military officers," writes Governor Winthrop, confessed their delusion before the Court, "and so blessed God that had so timely discovered their errour and danger to them."

Recantation saved them. But once again, as when she stood on trial before the Court, the words of her own mouth, prompted by her proud spirit, unafraid, proved Anne Hutchinson's undoing.

XVIII

EXCOMMUNICATION

Again the stage was set in the Boston meetinghouse. Again it was early forenoon. Again members of the Boston church who had laid aside their work for the day crowded the bare room. As many nonmembers and visitors from other towns as could be packed into the small edifice were there. The ministers of the whole colony were there. Court was over and the magistrates were there. Elder Leverett presided, but Pastor Wilson put the motion.

They read again the errors of which they accused Anne Hutchinson. Then, amid a solemn hush, the arraigned woman rose and with bent head, in a very low voice quite unlike her usual confident and forcible delivery, she read her recantation. She acknowledged that she had erred, that God had withdrawn his countenance from her because she had underrated his ordinances, slighting both the magistrates and the elders. Moreover, she admitted that at the time of her trial before the Court, she had considered only what she could criticize in the magistrates' proceedings without respecting their authority. What she had said about her revelations was rash and ungoverned.

In short, she was heartily sorry that anything she had said had drawn any away from listening to the elders of the colony. She would fain have the church pray for her.

It was an excellent recantation, though a little hedged about with provisos, but it was audible to only those who sat in the front seats. The elders were not satisfied that so few should have the privilege of hearing their erring sister acknowledge her mistakes. The presiding officer asked that someone read it again so that the whole congregation could hear it.

This duty naturally fell to Cotton. In his clear voice, he repeated the heads of her "groce and fundatmentall errours" and her confession that all she had done she did through a pride of spirit. This time, the whole congregation heard without difficulty. It seemed to make a clean breast of the affair. Winthrop says that "thus far the assembly conceived hope of her repentance."

But at this very instant, exactly as she had turned the Court at Newtowne against her at the moment when she might have been saved, so again she did with her church. There was this difference, at Newtowne she had spoken gratuitously, prompted by her own elation. This time, tired, ill, and with child, she would have kept silent if the ministers had let her alone. John Wilson took the lead.

There is explanation for Wilson's attitude in what he

had suffered at her hands in the past. We must remember that he had been obliged actually to fight for his parish while this quick-tongued, clever disputant turned his people against him and baited him in his own pulpit. Now he said that her recantation was incomplete because it still left in doubt the veracity of Mr. Shepard and the other ministers who had labored with her in Roxbury. This refers to the moment when she had interrupted Cotton's admonition the week before, to say that she never held the opinions of which they accused her until she went to Roxbury.

Meekly, Anne replied that she had spoken rashly and unadvisedly. She did not mean to slight either the ministers or the Scriptures, or anything that was set up of God. If Mr. Shepard thought she had any such purpose in her mind he was deceived.

Unfortunately, Mr. Shepard, usually so "sweet-affecting and soul-ravishing," was now deeply offended. He might call her a liar, but he objected to a retort in kind. Not at all satisfied with her apology, he insisted that she could not turn off her gross errors by simply saying, "You misunderstood me." "I fear it doth not stand with true repentance," said he.

Thereupon ensued a perplexing four-cornered conversation among Cotton, Shepard, Eliot, and Anne in regard to what really was said or not said in those Roxbury colloquies. They were especially concerned as to whether or not Anne Hutchinson "had denied that there were no Graces inherent in Christ himself." The scribe who took shorthand notes of this meeting and was able to understand them well enough to transcribe them into longhand afterwards is entitled to great respect. What Eliot and Shepard seemed to stand on was a determination to make her say absolutely and without reservation that she had held all of the seventeen or twenty-nine or thirty errors (reports differ as to the exact number) and that she now realized that they truly were errors and absolutely abjured them.

Other listeners added their questions, and finally so many of the ministers and magistrates assailed her that she lost her temper, which was never perfectly under control, and became stubborn. She took refuge behind the billows of argumentation in one sentence from which she could not be swept. "My judgment is not altered though my expression alters," she declared. In other words, "I think just as I always did whatever I may say."

That, of course, would never do at all. Of what good was her recantation when she took such ground? What kind of repentance was that? All her former adherents would see her holding stubbornly to her beliefs and would perceive that her recantation was only a formality.

John Wilson would not have it so. His temper was no better regulated than hers. He bluntly proclaimed, "The unruliness of this woman's tongue has been a great cause of this disorder, to set up herself, and draw disciples after her. She says one thing today and another to-morrow, and speaks falsely and ambiguously."

The others followed Wilson's lead. Dudley had no vote because he was not a member of the Boston church but of Roxbury. Nevertheless, he said, "Her repentance is in a paper. . . . And whether she had any help about it I will not enquire — [Decidedly a hit at Cotton!] but sure her repentance is not in her countenance." To which Peter added inelegantly, "I believe that she has vile thoughts of us, and thinks us to be nothing but a company of Jews." It was Peter who hit upon the real bone of contention when he said to her: "You have stept out of your place. You have rather been a husband than a wife, a preacher than a hearer, a magistrate than a subject, and so you have thought to carry all things in church and commonwealth as you would."

Pride, pride, pride! They never failed to taunt her with overwhelming ambition.

Shepard added his sweet-affecting note that she *never* had any true grace in her heart. "Yea, this day she hath shown herself to be a notorious imposter."

How surprised Cotton and Davenport must have been, after having coached her in her recantation, to see their submissive recusant calling forth this storm of opprobrium. How dazed Anne herself must have been, after having gone to church to make her peace, to find herself again the center of a whirlwind.

Her pride, her ambition, they could not forgive. Again and again they reiterated it and found it the root of her misconduct.

"One cause was," said Wilson, "to set yourself in the room of God, above others, that you might be extolled and admired and followed after, that you might be a great prophetess. I cannot but acknowledge that the Lord is just in leaving our sister to pride and lying. . . . I look at her as a dangerous instrument of the Devil raised up by Satan amongst us. . . . We should sin against God if we did not put away from us so evil a woman, guilty of such foul evils."

The ministers, exasperated, galled by her criticisms for so long a time, had lost their self-control. They vied with one another in pouring out the vials of their stored up hostility. "It is a wonderful wisdom of God," said Eliot, Apostle to the Indians, "to let her fall into such lies as she hath done this day, for she hath carried on all her errors by lies."

A lie! A lie! How they exulted in the word and all its synonyms. "Seducing to seduce, and deceiving to deceive, and lying to lie, and condemning authority and magistrates, still to condemn," said one of her adversaries. "God hath let her fall into a manifest lie," said Cotton. "Yea, to make a lie." Shepard seized upon the word and tortured it with precise distinctions, as between a sudden, unpremeditated falsehood and a deliberate fabrication with intent to deceive: "But now for one not to *drop* a lie, but to make a lie, and to maintain a lie!"

There was no hope for her. Once more she appealed to Cotton, saying, "Our teacher knows my judgment, for I never kept my judgment from him." "Yes," sneered Dudley, "I do remember she said she held nothing but what Cotton held."

However, Cotton would have no more of her. He had done his last for her when he had helped her prepare her recantation. His own escape had been far too narrow for him to attempt more. He did not, however, want the job of expelling her from the church. That was Wilson's task. Since her sin was lying rather than heresy, he argued, it was a question of morals rather than one of doctrine. Therefore, it fell not to the teacher who expounded doctrine, but to the pastor who taught the way of living, to pronounce the sentence of excommunication. Cotton was indeed glad of that.

A few members, among them her brother-in-law Richard Scott, timidly begged that they merely admonish her again in order that she might have a second chance. "She is distracted and cannot recollect her thoughts," Scott pleaded. But Cotton himself said, "Go on. She has lied." Richard Mather said go on. Leverett hesitated, and Dudley gave the deciding word now as he had done at the trial before the Court. Dudley cried, "She has been admonished in private many times. She should be driven from our midst."

Though Leverett presided, Wilson put the question. The question was whether all were of one mind that their sister should be cast out. No one spoke against it. The silence shut around her heart like ice. Not one voice among all those who had been her friends was raised in protest.

Then John Wilson's words of excommunication fell cold and pitiless upon the ears of the congregation and upon the numbed soul of Anne Hutchinson.

"In the name of the Lord Jesus Christ and in the name of the church I do not only pronounce you worthy to be cast out, but I do cast you out, and in the name of Christ I do deliver you up to Satan, that you many learn no more to blaspheme, to seduce, and to lie, and I do account you from this time forth to be a Heathen and a Publican, and so to be held of all the brethren and sisters of this congregation and of others: therefore I command you in the name of Christ Jesus and of this church as a leper to withdraw yourself out of the congregation."

A sigh swept over the rigid assembly. Anne Hutchinson turned, and alone, moved down the narrow aisle. . . . Outcast.

Even the ministers had no room for satisfaction, no room for any feeling but awe in the face of the appalling social and religious machinery that they had set in motion. Once or twice a sob broke beyond control from some overwrought woman. For the rest there was neither sound nor motion except the dull rustle of her garments and the weary fall of her footsteps on the sanded floor.

Then someone arose from her seat. A younger woman moved by Anne's side and passed through the door with her. Mary Dyer, afterwards hanged on Boston Common as a Quaker, now slipped her arm within that of her dear friend and mentor and helped her from the room.

A stranger was attending the trial as if it were one of the shows of the town. As the two women passed out of the church door, he pointed his finger at Mrs. Dyer and asked, "Who is that young woman?" Someone whispered,

"It is the woman that had the monster." So they brought a hushed secret to light. The previous October, just before they tried Anne Hutchinson at the General Court, poor Mary Dyer had suffered a miscarriage. Now, the magistrates and elders prosecuted a noisome investigation concerning her miscarriage. In consequence, the church admonished Mary Dyer's husband, just back from his trip to Rhode Island in search of a home, the next Sunday for maintaining "divers monstrous errors." The whole pitiful occurrence received nauseating publicity and was carefully recorded by Governor Winthrop in his "History." At the time of Mary Dyer's unfortunate delivery, Anne had been present to comfort and help. She kept the malformed birth a secret. This she did, she declared, on the advice of Cotton. It is consistent with his kindly nature that he did so advise her. The episode is additional proof that Anne was a kind of foster mother to the younger women of Boston. It shows that one of them, at least, had the gratitude and the courage to stand by her in adversity.

However, gratitude and courage were dangerous, as Mary Dyer and her husband soon found out.

As Anne Hutchinson passed from the church, one of the women said softly to her, "The Lord sanctify this unto you." Anne paused to reply, with the proud dignity that did not desert her in her bitterest hour, "The Lord judgeth not as man judgeth. Better to be cast out of the church than to deny Christ." These were her last public words in Boston.

So spoke young Francis Marbury to Bishop Aylmer and the High Commission Court: "I am to go whither it pleaseth God, but remember God's judgments!"

The Records of the First Church in Boston read:

"The 22nd of the first* month, 1638, Anne, the wife of our brother, William Hutchinson, having on the 15th of this month been openly, in the public congregation, admonished of sundry errors held by her, was on the same 22nd day cast out of the church for impenitently persisting in a manifest lie, then expressed by her in open congregation."

She who had been more sought after than any of the preachers was publicly proclaimed a liar.

That night, Anne slept in her own house. There was nothing now for Massachusetts to do with her except to see that she left its borders at the time specified.

---

* In the calendar then legally in use, the first month of the year was March.

XIX

REFUGE IN RHODE ISLAND

T he heads of the Massachusetts Colony considered their works and were pleased. "It was a happy day," wrote Winthrop, "to the church of Christ here and to many poor souls who had been seduced by her, who by what they heard and saw that day were (through the grace of God) brought off quite from her errors and settled again in the truth."

Thomas Weld continues the refrain:

"Thus it hath pleased the Lord to have compassion on his poor churches here, and to discover this great imposter, an instrument of Satan so fitted and trained to his service for interrupting the passage of His Kingdom in this part of the world, and poysoning the church here planted, as no story records the like of a woman since that mentioned in the Revelation."

A few years later another writer says, "Not any unsound, unsavorie or giddie fancie have dared to lift up his head or abide the light amongst us since Anne Hutchinson and her friends were banished."

Captain Roger Clap chimes in, "The snare is broken

and we and ours are delivered. . . . Now the churches had rest and were multiplied."

So the chorus rose. A period of religious uniformity ensued, and the ministers thanked God who had prospered their work. Nathaniel Ward wrote in his *Simple Cobbler of Agawam*: "I will petition to be chosen the universal idiot of the world if all the wits under the heavens can lay their heads together and find an assertion worse than this — that men ought to have liberty of conscience, and that it is persecution to debar them of it."

So tranquillity, or stagnation, prevailed in Massachusetts from the time of the expulsion of Anne Hutchinson until the Quaker troubles of the fifties. In that period of rest, the colony gained strength for its twenty years' persecution of the exponents of the doctrine of nonresistance.

As for Anne, she felt better now that the worst had happened. She proudly declared it the sweetest happiness, next to her faith in Christ, that ever befell her. She was *glad* to be gone from Massachusetts!

Her defeat was in actual effect a challenge to her, and the pride of which they had so often accused her now sustained her. To her enemies, this attitude could not look like anything but pure perversity. Amazed at the renewal of her spirits, they abhorred her seeming indifference to the vengeance of God. Did she think God would release what His church had bound? Surely He had given her up to her own hardness of heart. They shuddered at her callousness.

Yet where was Anne to go now? She might find it sweet to go, but whither? What should she do with the rest of her life? How best safeguard the future of those among her children whose youth constrained them to suffer with her?

Two or three days after her excommunication the magistrates notified her that her sentence of banishment was to go into effect by the end of the month. In the brief interim, she could stay in her own house but could not walk abroad. She swiftly set to work packing up what goods she and her children could convey with them. She engaged a boatman to take them down the bay to Wollaston, to her husband's farm. A tablet in "Anne Hutchinson Square," near the Wollaston depot, across the bridge over the railroad, now approximately indicates the place where she tarried. On the adjoining property, William's sister Mary Wheelwright was still living with her mother. Mary and her family were getting ready to start north to join Wheelwright, who had gone to New Hampshire. Anne's original plan had been to go with them. To change that plan, came her son Edward with word from his father. William had found a home for her on the island of Aquidneck, not many miles from Providence where Roger Williams was settled.

So Anne set forth with her family for Aquidneck in that backward spring of 1638, to make the sixty-mile trip overland by way of Providence. It was a good six days' journey. The traveling in the first week of April was along trails made muddy with spring freshets. Anne was in delicate health and there were other women and several children in the party, to make the going slow.

Her son Francis, a youth of eighteen, Bridget and Samuel, Anne, Maria, Katherine, together with the small ones, William, Susan and two-year-old Zuryell went with Anne. Richard, one of the older Hutchinson sons, is supposed to have stayed behind in Boston: he is next heard of in London. Edward Hutchinson and some of the other Aquidneck explorers acted as guides.

Whenever they could, the travelers put up for the night at the house of some settler in the wilderness, but many times it was not possible. There were forests penetrated only by Indian trails and there were rivers crossed only by canoe. It was a journey more than difficult, even dangerous, but in time Anne arrived at her destination and the comforting arms of her husband.

William Hutchinson and his companions were clearing ground and building homes. They were busily putting into operation a project that had been in their minds for several months.

Long before the disarming, disfranchising, and banishing of those who signed the Boston Petition, some of the more radical members of the colony had gathered at Coddington's house. There, they discussed the possibility of finding a freer home for themselves. With so much land available, why stay where they were balked and hampered? They wanted good soil, water, and wood. They wanted relief from what seemed to them the violent extremities of temperature on Massachusetts Bay. Above all, they wanted freedom from interference with their religious life. Two weeks before Anne's excommunication, on March 7, 1638, nineteen men met, probably at Coddington's house, and subscribed their names to an agreement. It began with these words:

"We whose names are underwritten do solemnly in the presence of Jehovah incorporate ourselves into a Bodie Politick."

First to sign was William Coddington, then John Clarke, physician, defender of liberty of conscience, and later founder of the Baptist Church in Newport. The third name on the list was that of William Hutchinson. Each of the three on whom the responsibility of the project especially rested fortified his signature with a Biblical reference. William's was 2 Kings 11:17: "And Jehoida made a covenant between the Lord and the King and the people, that they should be the Lord's people: between the King also and the people."

Edward Hutchinson the elder, and Edward Hutchinson the younger, Thomas Savage, William Coggeshall, William Aspinwall, William Baulston, and Mary Dyer's husband William — these are some of the other familiar names on the roll. At least twelve of the signers were members of the Boston church, and sixteen were among those whom they disarmed for signing the Petition. When they incorporated, they appointed William Coddington to be sole magistrate with the title of judge.

They at once dispatched a committee of the chief men to find a place of settlement. Their original intention was to search as far as Long Island or even New Jersey. However, Roger Williams persuaded them to stop at the island of Aquidneck. Now called the island of Rhode Island, Aquidneck extended about fifteen miles north and south. The Seaconnet River divided it from the mainland on the east, on the west by Narragansett Bay. Its climate was a little more even than that of Massachusetts Bay. Its contour level, it promised easy cultivation. Coddington, in the name of his associates and with the assistance of Roger Williams, bought it from the sachems* Miantonomo and Canonicus for forty fathoms of white beads and some small benefices to local chiefs. Williams wrote afterwards that "it was not price or money that could have purchased Rhode Island, but 'twas obtained by that love and favour which that honored gentleman, Sir Harry Vane and myself, had with the great sachem Miantonomo."

Coddington and the others went back to Boston to arrange their affairs. Then reenforced by several more men who had come under the Massachusetts ban, they established early in the spring a permanent settlement at Pocasset, which they later called Portsmouth. Here William Hutchinson was industriously making preparations for the coming of his dear ones.

This was the newborn colony, lodged in tents and huts on the northeastern end of the island, to which Anne arrived about the middle of April. She was tired out with the journey, worn by the ordeals through which she had passed during the fall and winter. It is no wonder that she soon fell seriously ill and suffered an unhappy outcome of her pregnancy.

Dr. Clarke told Governor Winthrop that after she

---

* Sachems: North American Indian chiefs.

reached her new home, some six weeks before her delivery, she consulted him, "feeling her body to be greatly distempered and her spirits failing, and in that regard doubtful of her life."

Poor lady! Who can wonder?

What does give cause for wonder is the immense public concern that Boston took in her illness. Not that they expressed sympathy. Far from it! Mr. Cotton, made her misfortune the subject of a sermon that he preached on lecture day. He drew an edifying parallel between the unnatural birth of which she had been delivered and the erroneous ideas which she held. Governor Winthrop was so much impressed by the providential coincidence that he wrote to Dr. Clarke for a fuller account of the case. When he received the report, he duly recorded it in his "History," *ad nauseam.*

The subject seemed to fascinate Winthrop. A little later he discovered still further details in conversation with Dr. Clarke. Winthrop passed them on to Cotton, who in turn transmitted them to his congregation. Cotton carefully corrected some mistakes that he made in his former sermon and referred to a letter from the lady's husband as the source of his original information.

It must indeed have been a worthy means of grace to the Boston church! Nevertheless, it is only fair to Cotton and Winthrop to remember that they thought they saw one of God's providences in this affliction of a heretic. Winthrop was one of those who objected most firmly to hearing Anne Hutchinson talk about "providences." Nevertheless, he continually records omens and portents whereby he believed that God showed His pleasure or His displeasure — more particularly the latter.

Mention has already been made of a like misfortune suffered by beautiful, ill-fated Mary Dyer, who dared to walk out of church with Anne directly after the sentence of excommunication had been uttered. Mary Dyer's "monstrous birth" was also carefully and circumstantially recorded in Winthrop's "History." In a preface to the *Short Story of the Rise, Reign and Ruin of the Antinomians* Thomas Weld solemnly draws a lesson from this pitiful concurrence of calamities:

"Thus God himself," Weld piously concludes, "was pleased to step in with His casting voice, and bring His own vote and suffrage from Heaven, by testifying His displeasure against their opinions and practices, as clearly as if He had pointed with His finger, in causing these two fomenting women, in the time of the height of the opinions, to produce out of their wombs, as before they had out of their brains, such monstrous births as no chronicle (I think) hardly ever recorded the like.

"He that runs may read their sin in their judgments."

Truly the Puritans thought their God moved in a mysterious way His wonders to perform! But they were not alone in their superstitions, nor have these died out. Handed down from those early days when men tried the merits of a case by force of combat, the faith in omens took on a religious aspect in Puritan days. In modern times, it masquerades as a half-mocking, half-fearful gesture of obeisance to Luck.

In this scandal mongering in Boston we can see the source of that silly entry made several years later in the British Colonial Papers. We refer to the gossip concerning Anne Hutchinson and Mary Dyer, to the effect that they came over with Sir Harry Vane and that "he desbauched them both and both were delivered of monsters."

Their ignorance of female physiology is only equal to the malice of the writers.

At Portsmouth, Anne was the leading spirit, though we properly call Coddington the father of the new colony. He was strongest in money, birth and experience, but it was by reason of his persistent support of Anne Hutchinson that they had driven him to leave Massachusetts. Spiritually, Anne dominated Portsmouth, certainly at the beginning. In numbers, too, the Hutchinsons predominated. There were William and Anne and their children.

There was William's brother Edward with his family; a few months later there came another brother, Samuel. William received several grants of land for himself and for his children between Town Pond and Great Cove. The house where William and Anne lived stood, if tradition is accurate, near a fork in the old main road just south of Town Pond. It is interesting to note that they gave no deeds of the early grants of land. The Indian deed to the island was in Coddington's name. The guarantee of the ownership of the individual settlers was merely in the entries made in the town record.

When Anne arose from her sickbed and looked about her, she found Portsmouth to be a place where she could at last draw a free breath. How long it would stay so she could not tell.

XX

THE ISLE OF ERRORS

Politically, Portsmouth was a place of free and simple government. Theologically, it was a place for the free expression of religious opinion. "No one shall be accounted a delinquent for doctrine," they voted on the same day that they agreed upon a democracy, "provided it be not repugnant to the government or laws established." Not quite as elastic as Roger William's settlement at Providence, which granted religious liberty to all men, even the heathen, Aquidneck admitted all that were Christians. Anne, who was as fastidious as anyone about opinions, could not have agreed with all that she heard expressed in her new home. Nevertheless, she certainly rejoiced in her own freedom. "The Isle of Errors," Massachusetts called Aquidneck; it was, at any rate, a place of free speech.

Here Anne resumed the position that she had held in Boston society before her catastrophe. A tiny court of friends and kinsmen surrounded her. She was a preacher; perhaps, for a while, she was *the* preacher. Edward Johnson committed a good many inaccuracies in his *Wonder-Working Providence* and his prejudices often colored his statements. Yet other reports corroborate his exactness when he says that Anne Hutchinson preached. "Some of the female sexe preached at Aquidneck," he wrote. "Especially the grand mistresse of them all, who ordinarily prated every Sabbath day, till others thirsted after honour in the same way with herselfe, drew away her auditors and then she withdrew herselfe . . . to a more remote place."

At one of her meetings, when she and her companions were at prayer, an earthquake which visited New England that year shook the house. The little structure trembled, the earth rocked and rippled beneath them. What wonder that to some of those enthusiastic souls it seemed like a visitation from Heaven, and that the Holy Ghost was literally and visibly descending upon them as upon the apostles of old! What wonder, too, that John Winthrop, hearing of this delusion, was all the more convinced of the madness of "revelations." Yet he, too, wrote hardly a page of his "History" without recording what seemed to him one of God's providences. What was a providence to one was merely an accident to another, according to his bent.

It cannot be denied that the Rhode Island settlement did attract the erratic as well as the sanely liberal. The saying was that if a man was too good for Massachusetts he went to Connecticut, if he was too bad he went to Rhode Island. Hence, "The Isle of Errors."

Anne and her friends had hoped to get Harry Vane back. Roger Williams wrote to Winthrop: "I find their longings great after Mr. Vane, although they think he cannot return this year. The eyes of some are so earnestly fixed upon him that Mrs. Hutchinson professeth if he come not to New she must to Old England. I have endeavored by many arguments to beat off their desires of Mr. Vane as G. G. [Governor-General] and the chief are satisfied unless he come so for his life, but I have endeavored to show the snare in that also."

How satisfying for Anne if her enthusiastic young friend had established himself in her new, secluded retreat!

It was not long before disagreements began to creep into this Paradise. Early in the second year, Coddington and his assistants, desiring a more aristocratic government, withdrew to form a new settlement at Newport. They took with them a few men of birth and property and the colony records.

Two days before the separation, those who intended to stay drew up another pact. A photostat of the remnants of this pact in the town archives at Portsmouth shows William Hutchinson's neat and precise signature at the head. Then comes Brother Samuel's. Several of the men could sign only by making their mark. The pact acknowledged allegiance to King Charles and subscribed to trial by jury according to English law. In both these items it differed from the theocratic system of government by "the Word of God," proclaimed by the other New England colonies. William Hutchinson was chosen judge with eight assistants.

John Winthrop in his "History" makes two entries in this connection: "At Aquiday, also, Mrs. Hutchinson exercised publickly, and she and her party (some three or four families) would have no magistry"; and, "At Aquiday the people grew very tumultuous, and put out Mr. Coddington and the three other magistrates, and chose Mr. William Hutchinson only, a man of a very mild temper and weak parts, and wholly guided by his wife, who had been the beginner of all the former troubles in the country, and still continued to breed disturbances."

The break did not last long. A year later the two settlements united under Coddington as Governor, and William Hutchinson was made one of his assistants. Newport became the more important town, but the Portsmouth idea persisted in the democratic form of government.

Robert Baylie, in his *Dissuasive from the Errors of the Time*, says he had Roger Williams's word for it that

Anne Hutchinson persuaded her husband to resign his position as Assistant after one year, "because of the opinion, which newly she had taken up, of the unlawfulness of magistry." If both Baylie and Williams were right, then Anne had gone the entire limit of liberalism and arrived at anarchy. Perhaps in her sequestered wilderness she had come to believe, as other idealists have done, that in a perfect state man is governed only by his own sense of right, and that magistrates were no more necessary in Aquidneck than in the Garden of Eden. She was supremely convinced that the Christian held within his own breast the assurance of salvation, that the Spirit dwelt within him. For such persons magistrates were obviously superfluous. As for the others, they were to be converted, not coerced. That was simple and clear. So perhaps it is true that she would not let William run for office again.

Even if Anne held this opinion about magistrates, Portsmouth and Newport did not, for they kept on having them.

Both the political and the religious state of Aquidneck troubled Massachusetts, particularly the latter. The Boston church felt responsible for those of its members who had gone away. Anne Hutchinson's opinions were still a bugbear. The records of the church and court bristle with allusions to them. They remained the pet horror of the colony until Quakerism gave them something still more disturbing to think about. They fined and they whipped and they exiled those who showed any spark of heretical opinion. Five years later they executed Robert Potter "whose sins were first in the time of Mrs. Hutchinson, when divers of our church were seduced to familisme and scizme." They saw a Providence of God in the death of "Mrs. Mary Dummer, a godly woman, but by the seduction of some of her acquaintances she was led away into the new opinions in Mrs. Hutchinson's time. She dyed in a most uncomfortable manner with risings in the mouth and other vyolences of nature."

They rejected the Reverend Mr. Knolles, "a weak minister lately come out of England," for holding some of Anne Hutchinson's opinions. The death of the barber-surgeon who perished in a snowstorm on the way from Boston to Roxbury, whither he had been summoned to pull a tooth, was an act of God, said the Puritans. For the tooth-puller "had been more than ordinary laborious to draw men to these sinful errors, that were formerly so frequent and are now so newly overthrown."

By December, eight months after Anne's departure from Boston, they had not yet obliterated her doctrine. Families were still divided and feuds had been created that were destined to last many years. On December 13, they declared a Fast Day on account of the prevailing sickness and heresies "and the general declining of professors to the world." At this time, Mr. Cotton preached a sermon that reviewed the whole matter and gave him an opportunity to vindicate his own part in it. He said that those whom they had banished had imputed words to him that he never uttered. They had made him to serve as a cloak for their opinions and that they had deserved banishment. However, he thought it best not to send any more away but to put in prison those who persisted and reason with them. He clearly felt that exile was making Hutchinsonianism altogether too attractive to certain enthusiastic souls.

On the other hand, Anne in her Rhode Island retreat was equally concerned for her former fellow members in the Boston church and felt equally responsible for them. She could not forgive herself if she neglected her Christian duty of watch and ward over those who went astray. Therefore, she proceeded gravely to admonish the Boston church and to that effect wrote them a letter. Her letter never reached its full destination. The elders held it up, having decided that since she was an excommunicated person, it was out of order to read her communication to the meeting.

"By these examples," observed Winthrop, "we see how dangerous it is to slight the censures of the church, for it was apparent that God had given them up to strange delusions."

As he received news, more or less unreliable, from the new settlement, he heard that those who had gone with Anne Hutchinson were falling into new errors daily, one of them to the effect that women have no souls. That surely was a belief of which no one could accuse Anne, inherent feminist that she was. The fact was that no speculation was too wild to be attributed by Massachusetts to their recalcitrant brothers and sisters in Rhode Island.

The Boston church now proceeded to perform its own duty of watch and ward. To them it seemed an act of the most arrant effrontery for the Rhode Islanders to pretend to establish a church of their own. Some of the members of the Newport and Portsmouth congregations were persons who had never belonged to any other church on this side of the Atlantic. Well and good. But others were members of the Boston and Roxbury churches who had been either publicly admonished or cast out. Still others were members in good standing who had accompanied the exiles for family reasons. On these the parent churches felt that they still had a hold and for these they felt a responsibility. According to the Massachusetts idea, any church established by such persons was formed in a disorderly way. The regular or orderly way was to get permission from the parent church to form a new one, and such permission the Boston church would never grant if excommunicated members were to be included.

After having vainly written to their Rhode Island members, especially to Coddington, and endeavored to call them to account, the Boston church finally resolved to send a committee to reason with those willful ones. The committee was made up of Captain Edward Gibbons, William Hibbins, and John Oliver, Jr., all of whom had been on more or less friendly terms with Anne Hutchinson.

The committee went and returned, having their journey for their pains. On March 16, 1640, at the close of Mr. Cotton's sermon, they told the story of their venture into the Antinomian wilds.

They had made a hard and dangerous journey in midwinter through the forests and across streams into Rhode Island. Arriving there, they went first to Newport, where after some demur the people there gave them a formal hearing and returned a satisfactory answer.

At Portsmouth, the stronghold of the Hutchinson family, they had poorer success. Deacon Coggeshall's house was their first port of call and his generous hospitality gave them some hope. But their hope was vain.

When they asked him to arrange a meeting where their letters might be read, he showed a streak of iron. "What power," he inquired, "hath one church over another? The letters cannot be presented except as from the Boston church to ours. Yet you deny the existence of any church here."

That was an impasse. By the terms of their instructions the Boston committee could not treat with the Portsmouth people as a separate church, but as unruly members of the Boston church. Hence the only thing they could do was to take the letters around from home to home.

First, as was proper, they called on Judge William Hutchinson, making it clear that their errand was with him and not his wife. To him they brought messages of good will and an urgent prayer that he confess his sins and renounce the doctrines of his wife. William had few words of reply, but they entirely covered the situation. "That I shall not do," said William. "I am more nearly tied to my wife than to the church, and I look upon her as a dear saint and servant of God."

Disappointed at the contrariness of this supposedly mild and gentle man, they decided to talk with the lady.

Anne swept into the room and seated herself in the master's chair. Here were old acquaintances, and she showed them courtesy, but no more. They told their mission, to bring word from the Lord and from their church.

"There be lords many and gods many, but I acknowledge but one Lord," she said. "Which lord do you mean?"

This was no auspicious beginning. The woman had started asking questions as usual. They stiffened their dignity and replied, "We come in the name of but one Lord, that is God."

"Then we agree so far," she admitted promptly, adding with sarcasm, "And where we do agree let it be set down." She remembered that of old their supposed agreements had a fashion of slipping away.

"We have a message from the church of Christ at Boston," Captain Gibbons continued.

"The church of *Christ* at Boston?" she inquired, raising her brows. "I know of but one church in Boston."

Messrs. Gibbons, Hibbins, and Oliver digested this devastating remark and with commendable patience defended the divine institution of their church. However, the scripturally learned lady refused to acknowledge the Boston church as a church of Christ. Finally, smarting under the remembrance of the treatment that she had received before the tribunal of that church — cast out, shunned as if she bore contagion — she arose in her passionate pride and bade the emissaries of Boston to depart from her house. Unfriendly historians say that with strong language she bade them begone. They say, to be specific, that she called the Boston church a whore and a strumpet. Perhaps she did. She was born in the days of good vituperative Queen Bess.

Anne's son Francis was the next Hutchinson to occupy the attention of the Boston church. Francis seems to have been more like his mother than any of the other children. He had gone to Rhode Island with her and had applied to the Boston church for a letter of dismissal on the ground that he had to live with his parents. They refused it. John Cotton's answer addresses young Francis as "our beloved brother at Aquethick," and mentions "a good report of his constancy in the truth and the faith of the gospel." Nevertheless, it does not release him from his membership in the Boston church. It hardly could, since Boston did not recognize the church on Aquidneck as any church at all.

Next, son Edward comes to the fore. During that autumn of 1640 the Rhode Island people rejected still another attempt on the part of Boston to reclaim its brands from the burning. The Reverend John Wilson, quite swept off his feet by his anger at their continued hardness of heart, cried from his pulpit, "There is nothing for it but to let them be to the church as heathen!" However, even then one of those troublesome Hutchinsons opposed him. This time, Edward. To John Wilson consigning Aquidneck root and branch to the realm of heathendom, young Hutchinson rose to make a polite objection:

"I would not have my silence wrap up my consent with that of the brethren," said he. "As I would not condemn the church or the commonwealth, so I would not justify all that is done."

"You lay yourself open to suspicion," Wilson warned him sternly. "Either you should have been silent, or you should tell what your objections are. If you do not justify the proceedings of the church and commonwealth, you cast reproach upon them and censure them, which you ought not to do, for both church and commonwealth dealt justly in casting out your mother."

(There was this good thing about Wilson, that one always knew just where he stood.)

Edward Hutchinson answered that he desired to speak no particulars, only he could not approve or consent to all that had been done. He was one of the unlucky ones, lovers of moderation, who can always see both sides of a question. Neither wholly approving nor wholly disapproving of his mother's course, he did his best for the family. He looked after his father's affairs in Boston, and in July 1639, applied for permission to sell the house where his parents had lived to his rich uncle Richard, linen draper of London. They granted permission. The house stood until the fire of 1711.

Two others of Anne's family were not as politic as Edward. One was young Francis again, still running true to the name of his grandfather Francis; the other was Anne's son-in-law, William Collins.

Collins was a young minister, originally out of Gloucester, England, more recently of Saint Christopher or Barbados, where he had suffered for nonconformity. He taught school for a while in Hartford, then heard of Anne Hutchinson's doctrines and went to Rhode Island to learn more about them. There he became enamoured of her doctrines, or of her daughter, and stayed. He became a zealous convert and married the daughter. Thereupon he wrote a lively letter to Boston, charging all the Massachusetts churches and ministers with being anti-Christian, and calling the King of England, King of Babylon. In short, Collins was both anti-clerical and anti-monarchical.

In the summer of 1641 the two youthful enthusiasts, Francis Hutchinson and William Collins, went to Boston looking for trouble. They found it. They were arrested and taken before the Governor, sitting in state with his

Council and the elders of the church. They arraigned Collins for his letter, Francis for bad language. (He had, in fact, called the Boston church a strumpet, perhaps having heard the epithet so applied at home.) The young men were fined lavishly, Collins a hundred pounds, Francis fifty, and were put in prison until such time as they could pay. The reason given for the excessive fines was the desire of the authorities to keep them shut up for a good long time, and the fact that the Hutchinson family had already cost the state at least five hundred pounds "for the Synod and other things." But winter came on, the prison was inconvenient, and the young men would not attend church unless dragged thither by main force. In order to end a bad matter Boston abated their fines, let them be their own bondsmen, and dismissed them. They forbade them, on pain of death, to appear in the Bay Colony again. Still true to form, the Hutchinsons caused contention. Some in the church sympathized with Francis and his brother-in-law. The constable who had charge of them was fined because he had been too lenient with them.

Besides all this, and in spite of everything that Massachusetts could do, Anne continued to teach and exhort in her Rhode Island retreat. Roger Williams, who became acquainted with her, said that he knew much good of her. The Rhode Island settlements prospered, but it is certain that considerable dissension attended their history, as needs must be where tongues are free to wag. However, it was a healthy dissension, more healthy than the enforced unanimity of the Bay Colony.

In 1642 came Anne's great personal grief when William died. He was fifty-six years old. "A very honest and peaceable man of good estate," wrote John Winthrop magnanimously, — wishing, no doubt, that the peaceable man had not been too peaceable to control his own wife.

It is a decent obituary, that given by Winthrop. However, it takes no account of William's endurance of troubles by land and by sea. It says nothing of his patience under disappointments and harassments, of his willingness to let Anne stand first. Good William!

William's widow now gathered her seven younger children about her and started forth on the last stage of her wanderings.

XXI

THE JOURNEY'S END

Anne on the move again!

It may be that she was tired of queer beliefs, all freely expressed. For that attitude of mind in Portsmouth and that liberality of speech, though not for all the beliefs, Anne was herself largely responsible. However, it is quite possible that religious controversy, which was once the breath of life to her, became less satisfying. She was growing older and now her party held the reins of government. Authority proverbially turns radicals into conservatives. Or it may be that with her patient and provident husband gone, she desired above all things some place of peace where she could bring up her children.

Her chief reason for moving, however, was the threat of interference from her old foes. She saw unmistakable evidence that Massachusetts meant to include Rhode Island within its jurisdiction if it could in any way be accomplished. No excuse was too slight to be seized upon by the Bay Colony for extending its control over the towns settled by its outcasts. It is easy to see why Anne

Hutchinson was averse to coming again under the authority of the Massachusetts Court, with the clergy sitting enthroned behind it.

Especially had she cause for dread when she heard that they were accusing her in Boston of practicing witchcraft. "Why not?" said her old enemies. She consorts with Jane Hawkins, a notorious sorcerer. She has won over by some mysterious means that scholarly young minister William Collins who had warned others against her teachings. Collins had written from Hartford to his friend Hale urging him to beware the influence of Anne Hutchinson. Yet "being come to Mrs. Hutchinson, he was also taken with her heresies and in great admiration of her so as these, and other the like before when she dwelt at Boston, gave cause of suspicion of witchcraft, for it was certainly known that Hawkins' wife (who continued with her and was her bosom friend) had much familiarity with the devil in England, when she dwelt at Saint Ives, where divers ministers and others resorted to her and found it true." (The rumor was that at the Portsmouth meetings, Jane Hawkins would sometimes fall into a trance and exhort in the Latin tongue. If this is true, Anne's keenly critical mind must have been either dulled or nauseated.) Governor Winthrop seemed unable to distinguish between a magnetic personality and witchcraft. What magic there was lay in the pretty eyes of Anne's young daughter whom Collins wooed and wed.

For several reasons, then, Anne clearly saw that there was no sure prospect of safety in Rhode Island. Her sentence of banishment would include Rhode Island if they should ever recognize it as a part of the Bay Colony. It was better for her to leave before she was compelled to. Thomas Weld slightingly observed, "Mrs. Hutchinson being weary of Rhode Island, or rather the Island being weary of her, departed from thence with all her family."

Her family now was somewhat reduced in number. Edward was back in Boston, troubled by the continual calumnies heaped upon his kindred. However, he was in decent standing in the Boston church, though objecting in later years to the persecution of Quakers and Baptists. He did his best to look after his father's Massachusetts property. He became captain in the militia and was wounded at Brookfield in King Philip's War, died on the way home at Marlboro, and was buried there. His great-grandson Thomas Hutchinson was the last royal deputy-governor of Massachusetts and the author of a history of the colony.

Anne's next younger son Richard did not share his mother's later wanderings. By 1645 he was evidently back in England, for in that year the Boston church lovingly dismissed him to the church of Dr. Thomas Godwin in London.

Faith Hutchinson, wife of Thomas Savage, continued to live in Boston. Savage had been one of the disarmed signers of the Boston Petition, had subscribed to the Portsmouth Covenant, and had spoken up boldly for his mother-in-law at her church trial. Nevertheless, he made his peace with Boston and stayed there, becoming wealthy and influential. He was commander-in-chief of the Massachusetts forces in King Philip's War. When Faith died, he married for his second wife a daughter of the Reverend Mr. Symmes of Charlestown, one of the most active opponents of Anne Hutchinson.

Another of the Hutchinson girls, Bridget, whom they named for her Grandmother Marbury, married John Sanford, also one of the signers of the Boston Petition and the Portsmouth Covenant. She lived in Rhode Island until the death of her husband, then came back to Boston and was married to Major Phillips.

Samuel Hutchinson, who was a youth of eighteen when his mother left Portsmouth, is supposed to have remained in Rhode Island.

The rest of the sons and daughters, the gallant Francis, who was now twenty-two, Anne, Mary, Katherine, William, Susan and Zuryell, the one Boston-born child, now six years old, accompanied their mother on her third pilgrimage. With them also went William Collins and several other Rhode Island families.

Anne first stopped her company at Long Island. They had already made settlements along the northern shore of the island. Some by the Dutch, some by men from Connecticut and Massachusetts, made restless by hard times, and some by families from Rhode Island, ever seeking new frontiers. Winthrop says that the Governor (of the Dutch) invited them by fair offers. One of the most important settlements was that of Lady Deborah Moody, chief among the Baptists. Lady Moody herself was another *dux femina*.* Though daughter of the Earl of Lincoln and sister of Lady Arbella Johnson and Lady Susan Humphrey, she had been expelled from the church at Salem for her Baptist beliefs and had gone to the region of Gravesend on the western end of Long Island. Her excommunication did not prevent her from attracting many to her settlement. She built a palisaded house and had many stout henchmen to defend it against the Indians. In later years Governor Stuyvesant highly regarded her and gave her the privilege of choosing the magistrates of Gravesend. Her personal popularity reconciled the people of the town to this arbitrary

---

* Dux femina: feminine leader. (Latin.)

infringement of their freemen's rights.

On Long Island, some distance north of Lady Deborah's homestead, Anne first established herself. There, according to Thomas Weld, "at Astoria opposite the place called Hell-gate, this woful woman" met her end. However, Mr. Weld was mistaken. Fascinated by the appropriateness of the name Hell-Gate and not well acquainted with the geography of the locality, he did not take into account the last removal of all that she had made.

This final removal was to the mainland on what is now the extreme southeastern part of the State of New York on the shore of Pelham Bay. Near Split Rock in beautiful Pelham Bay Park is the spot where Anne spent her last days. A stream which divides Pelham from East Chester and forms one of the boundaries of Pelham Bay Park still bears the name Hutchinson River. A point of land jutting into the bay is by tradition called Anne's Hoeck, though the exact origin of that name is shrouded in legend.

Not far away were two other English families, the Throckmortons and the Cornhills. From the Cornhill family (later spelled Cornell) was descended the founder of Cornell University. Throckmorton, a friend of Roger Williams, had accompanied Williams from England to Salem and followed him to Providence. He became a Baptist and with some others of the same persuasion settled east of Bronck's Land and called his place Vreedenland, Land of Peace. Next to him settled Thomas Cornhill and beyond him Anne Hutchinson.

"These people," wrote Winthrop, "had cast off ordinances and churches, and now at last their own people, and for larger accommodation had subjected themselves to the Dutch and dwelt scatteringly near a mile asunder."

A land of peace this domain of the liberal Dutch might be so far as freedom from religious persecution was concerned. However, a land of temporal peace it certainly was not. The years between 1641 and 1645 were years of havoc and terror in the Dutch colony and its environs. The Indians of the Hudson River tribes, infuriated by Dutch greed and deception, and supplied with Dutch firearms, had risen against the white man. From small beginnings the occasional forays had reached the proportions of warfare. White reprisals were followed by counter reprisals on the part of the redskins. The Dutch Governor bungled, the Dutch settlers fought with the fury of panic, the Indians were suspicious, vengeful, and sudden. A peace concluded through the good offices of De Vries was unfortunately not permitted to endure.

It was probably in the interval between hostilities that Anne Hutchinson and her companions moved from Long Island to the mainland. They tell the story that she engaged a certain James Sands to build her new home. Sands began work but became so uneasy on account of the Indians who lurked about, watching him from the woods, that he threw up his job. His energetic employer refused to be balked in her enterprise and secured the services of some less cautious carpenter who finished her house. Sometime in 1643 Anne and her family moved into their new, their ill-fated abode, and here Anne, with unfailing friendliness and missionary zeal, welcomed her Indian neighbors.

War broke out again. The River Indians alone had been engaged at first, but the Dutch settlers on Long Island, by their very terror and vindictiveness, roused the Island tribes. The second stage of the feud was worse than the first. Lady Deborah's palisaded home, so doggedly defended, was the only plantation left standing on western Long Island.

The Boston magistrates forbade Roger Williams to sail from Boston. Coming to New Amsterdam in order to sail for England he said: "my eyes saw the frights and the hurries of men, women and children, and the present removal of all that could to Holland."

In desperation the Dutch Governor called on the English captain, John Underhill, to help him out. (That attendant of Mars and Venus keeps turning up all along the coast for several years.) In spite of Underhill's assistance, there was continual bloodshed, burning of houses, cattle and barns, and even the Governor's guard was threatened. All who could, fled into the Dutch fort and not even there were they safe. Anne Hutchinson trusted the Indians. She neither feared nor sought refuge.

In John Winthrop's "History" appears the record of her last day:

"The Indians near the Dutch, having killed 15 men, as is before related, proceeded to begin to set upon the English who dwelt near the Dutch. They came to Mrs. Hutchinson in the way of friendly neighborhood, as they had been accustomed, and taking their opportunity killed her and Mr. Collins her son-in-law (who had been kept prisoner in Boston as before related) and all her family, and such of Mr. Throckmorton's and Mr. Cornhill's as were at home; in all sixteen, and put their cattle into their houses and burnt them."

Weld, with an eye to the providences of God, called this last act of tragedy, "a most heavy stroak upon herself and hers. . . . Some write that the Indians did burn her to death with fire, her house and the rest named that belonged to her; but I am not able to affirm what kind of death slew her, but slain it seems she is according to all reports. I never heard that the Indians in those parts did ever before commit the like outrage upon any one family or families, and therefore God's hand is the more apparently seen herein, to pick this woful woman, to make her and those belonging to her an unheard of example of their cruelty above others."

Ah, Mr. Weld!

Some of the Throckmortons and Cornhills managed to escape in a boat that came along at the very instant of the Indian attack. At least two of the men in the boat attempted to go to the rescue of those whom the Indians were assailing in their homes. The Indians killed these two and the boat withdrew with some of the women and children who had fled thither for safety.

Only one of the household on Anne's Hoeck, if that really is the spot, survived. This was the little girl Susanna, whom the Indians captured.

When they finally concluded another treaty of peace with the Indians in 1645, one of the articles insisted on a solemn obligation to restore the daughter of Anne Hutchinson. The Dutch guaranteed the ransom that had been offered by the New England friends of the little captive, and the obligation on both sides was fulfilled. Susanna was restored to the Dutch — against her will, it is said, since she had learned to like her Indian captors — and she was eventually returned to Rhode Island. She grew up and married John Cole of North Kingston, and became mother of the usual large family.

Among the rather doubtful traditions that have survived is one that in 1654 an Indian Sachem called Wampage, in signing a deed of land to Thomas Pell, for whom Pelham was named, designated himself Ann Hoeck. It was a custom among Indians to assume the name of a conspicuous person whom they had slain. Wampage is supposed thus to have signified his pride in having been the slayer of Anne Hutchinson.

The place looks safe enough today, yet hardly a retreat for the prophetess.

In perfectly enameled cars no less perfectly enameled women glide over impeccable roads. White villas gleam through smoothly pruned trees, suave lawns and gardens show nature well disciplined. A golf course, spruce and trim, offers recreation where white men and red once fought hand to hand.

Three hundred and fifty years ago the place was a wilderness with no cleared land except a few patches close to the three farmhouses scattered along the point at intervals of a mile.

Anne would have been past fifty, no older in years than many of the smartly-dressed, decorative matrons whose cars spin along the Shore Road today, but much older in appearance and in fact. Yet able to endure how much more! In the annals of the time, the farm was "Mrs. Hutchinson's place." She had not yet reached the point where she conceded the headship to son or son-in-law.

There were not many in the neighborhood for whom she could "exercise." However, the Throckmortons and the Cornhills would not have been in that particular spot if they had not felt some special attachment for her. It is probable that she was accustomed to expounding the Scriptures even in the company of the zealous young scholar who had married her daughter. The field of Christian listeners, however, was too limited for a woman of her teaching spirit. Like her friend Roger Williams, she entertained the hope of converting some of the heathen. So the Indians were in the habit of coming to her house "in the way of friendly neighborhood." There is no doubt that Anne, insofar as she could, explained to them the teachings of Christianity.

So, when two or three of the Indians appeared at the clearing that morning Anne welcomed them. "Tie up your dogs," the Indians said by sign, "for they have bitten some of us." Anne tied the dogs, gave the Indians water from her spring as they asked, and set before them the food that she and her daughters had prepared for the family.

Into the midst of this seeming friendliness came

William Collins and Francis Hutchinson, running from the fields to warn the women that dark forms crowded the point.

We hope the Indians made quick work of it. Under the assumption of friendliness the two or three decoys could easily appropriate the muskets and the small store of ammunition that stood by the cabin door. The dogs, although strong-hearted and strong of jaw, could not break their leashes.

Anne gathered her flock about her. Rapidly she counted them and with horror she realized that two were missing, her youngest two, Susanna and little Zuryell. They had gone out, as they often did, to pick berries in the thicket. All her summonses would be in vain, for how could they elude the cordon of the besiegers? Would God dim the eyes of the savages that they might not discover those little frightened forms? So little!

As it turned out, Susanna's fate was happier than that of the rest, but they made little Zuryell a horrifying sacrifice. Too frantic in her attempt to burrow into the thicket, she attracted the attention of an Indian. She was dragged back by the hair, haled to a tree stump in the clearing before the cabin, and there the tomahawk did its work. Susanna they did not find until later when they were slipping away as speedily as they came. They took her with them.

The cabin was no fort. The Indians were enraged by the high-handedness of the Dutch and seeking retaliation for the injuries inflicted upon them by the Mohawks at Dutch instigation. They were perhaps informed that the queen-like English woman was friend of the English warrior Underhill who had led the white band against them. Therefore, they resolved to wipe out this white settlement, along with all the others on the mainland and island. With arrow and tomahawk and the more terrifying weapon of fire, the Indians accomplished their purpose.

Without doing violence to history it is possible to continue from these recorded facts, and reconstruct more fully the piteous details of the tragedy.

The two young men, being fighters were disposed of first. Then it was easy to deal with the women and children.

Yet not so easy to deal with this prophetess. She was speaking magic. Solemn, sonorous, like the outpourings of their wise men, majestic speech flowed from her lips. She began by quoting from Psalm 91.

"I will say of the Lord, He is my refuge and my fortress; my God, in Him will I trust."

(That was the dirge that she raised in triumph for the death of her son William.)

"Surely He will deliver thee from the snare of the fowler, and from the noisome pestilence."

(Oh, where were Susanna and the little one?)

"Thou shalt not be afraid for the terror by night; nor for the arrow that flieth by day."

(Oh, Sue, Sue, bring back your sister, my little Sue!)

"A thousand shall fall by my side, and ten thousand at my right hand . . ." — ah, not my children, Lord! Not that! Yet the Lord giveth and the Lord taketh away. . .

Now she sought strength and hope from Psalm 94.

"They slay the widow and the stranger, and murder the fatherless. Yet they say, the Lord shall not see, neither shall the God of Jacob regard it."

There was her white lamb, her wee one — Oh-h-h! Her voice rose in an uncontrollable shriek. Her eyes were blinded with the hideous sight. She would rush to her child. A harsh hand gripped her shoulder. Her body stayed, unable to wrench itself away, but her spirit swept on. Now, if ever, God's Word must save. Exalted, unafraid, she chanted:

"Blessed is the man whom thou chastenest, O Lord. . . . In the multitude of my thoughts within me Thy comforts delight my soul. The Lord . . ."

"She is a witch-woman," said the Indians. "But her

magic doth not save her children. Her spirit hath deserted her. Now is the time to strike!"

Still, the voice rose in deathless faith. "The Lord is my defense, and my God . . . my God is the rock . . . of my . . . refuge."

They suffered her to speak no more.

Today men unrelaxed and intent, women manikin trim and self-possessed, glide in their shining cars over the sleek roads along Pelham Bay. A ceaseless, moving line, an uneasy throng, weary but unquenchable in their work and their play, what has Anne Hutchinson to do with them?

A restless spirit, a questioning mind, an energy that kept her in motion show the seventeenth-century prophetess to have been mother of the twentieth-century woman. More than that, she was a lonely exemplar in newborn America of that freedom of thought, word, and action that women now accept as unthinkingly as the air they breathe. She left a legacy — a legacy not even yet administered to its last jot and tittle.

EPILOGUE

THE SPIRIT OF ANNE SPEAKS

Mary Dyer, friend of Anne, became a Quaker* after Anne's death. The Massachusetts Bay Colony persecuted Quakers. Mary was tried and condemned to death by hanging on Boston Common; the entire community came to the event. Some agreed with the verdict of death; others, mostly women, secretly pitied the victim.

After the hanging, Mary's body was removed from the gallows, put into a cart, and taken to her home to be prepared for burial, and to be mourned by her family — husband and children.

That night, the spirit of Anne appeared in the quiet room. It spoke to the spirit of Mary Dyer, that was still hovering over the body.

"Oh, Mary, be ye comforted. Thy trials are over. Thy spirit can rejoice; it has shed thy body and this vale of tears.

"We have suffered intolerance and superstition in our lifetimes because of the ignorance of man. But our beloved Master asked us to forgive seventy times seven times. We are now free.

"Our life stories will be told to mankind in a distant future. They will be compassionate; they will understand.

"Someday, on these shores, a great nation will come into being. This land will enjoy a new birth of freedom. Women will drink of the freedom they deserve, given them by God. They will have the freedom to think, to speak out, to teach and preach. God has no favorites; He has created men and women equal, and new laws of the land will ordain freedom for women as well as men.

"Superstition will fade and intolerance will no longer be acceptable. Freedom of religion will prevail in this nation. Quakers and their beliefs will become highly respected and accepted, as well as other religions.

"No longer will women's talents be suffocated. The mind has no sex, and women have minds. Someday, the New Woman will be able to choose how many children she desires to bear and when. She will have great opportunities to develop her mind and spirit.

"A great, God-appointed woman will be born on these same shores, who will heal and teach both men and women, all over the world. Our sacrifice will have helped make this possible.

"The sex that gives birth to precious children — indeed, to mankind — is in no way inferior. Woman loves the offspring of her womb, bringing love to humanity.

" 'God is Love,' the disciple John said. God is also Life — the original source of all life. Woman corresponds to Life and to Love; hence, woman is more open and receptive to the awareness of the presence of God. Woman, with her nurturing love, given true equality can and will enrich our civilization. Unselfed love is the highest emotion that can be felt. This is why woman is not inferior. Those who engage in crime and war, the extremes of hatred, are the lowest types of mankind.

"Woman was not and is not the bringer of sin to mankind! The Book of Genesis errs! This false idea resulted in man's jealousy of women's power to give birth, and man blaming God and woman for his troubles, rather than taking responsibility for his own actions.

"Mary, I foresee what is ahead. Yes, a great nation will arise here, but a great crisis will occur for mankind, in the far future. Still, God prevails. Out of cataclysms and tribulation, a new race will arise. Woman will be the light bearer. The spirit of the coming age will be an age of peace and blossoming of the highest qualities and experience.

"Peace, Mary, peace. Be ye comforted. God loves you; you are truly one of His own. 'Forgive them, for they know not what they do', our Master said.

"Rest in the bosom of God, who is Good. In the future, God will be known by a new name — our own Father-Mother God. It must be so, because Humanity is made up of sons and daughters. God will be called 'She', as well as 'He.'

"I love you, Mary. I will guide you to your new, heavenly home!"

---

* Quakers: A religious sect founded by George Fox, of Leicestershire, England, about 1650, the members of which call themselves Friends. The name Quaker was applied in derision in 1650. Fox bade the judge to "tremble at the word of the Lord." The word had already been applied to a sect of religious enthusiasts and, according to some, was bestowed on the Friends because they really did tremble under the joy of religious emotion.

BIBLIOGRAPHY*

Adams, Brooks: The Emancipation of Massachusetts.

Adams, Charles Francis, *ed.*: Antinomians in the Colony of Massachusetts Bay.

Adams, Charles Francis: Three Episodes of Massachusetts History.

Adams, James T.: The Founding of New England.

Andrews, C. M.: Colonial Folk Ways.

Appleton, W. S., and Whitmore, W. H.: Record of Boston, Dorchester and Roxbury, in Reports of the Boston Record Commissioners.

Bell, Charles H.: Memoir of John Wheelwright. Prince Society Publications.

Bolton, Robert, Jr.: History of Westchester County.

Boston, Massachusetts: First Church Records.

Bryne, M. St. Clair: Elizabethan Life in Town and Country.

Callender, John: Centennial Sermon. Collections of Rhode Island Historical Society.

Chandler, Peleg W.: American Criminal Trials, vol. I.

Chapin, Howard M.: Documentary History of Rhode Island, vol. II.

Chester, J. L.: Hutchinson Ancestry.

Clap, Roger: Memoirs. Collections of Dorchester Antiquarian and Historical Society, no. I.

Clarke, John: Ill Newes from New-England. Massachusetts Historical Society, Collections, 4th series, vol. II.

Cotton, John: Way of the Congregational Churches Cleared.

Crawford, Mary Caroline; Old Boston in Colonial Days.

---

* Winnifred King Rugg, in the first edition, 1930, used the heading "Works Consulted in the Preparation of This Volume." She had done thorough research.

Dexter, Franklin P., *ed.*: Report of the Trial of Mrs. Anne Hutchinson before the Church in Boston. Massachusetts Historical Society, Proceedings, 2nd series, vol. IV.

Doyle, J. A.: Puritan Colonies, vol. I.

Drake, S. A.: History of Antiquities of Boston.

Drake, S. A., *ed.*: The Old Indian Chronicle.

Ellis, George E.: Life of Mrs. Anne Hutchinson, with a Sketch of the Antinomian Controversy. Jared Sparks, *ed.*

Ellis, George E.: Puritan Age and Rule in Massachusetts.

Fiske, John: Beginnings of New England.

Ford, W. C., *ed.*: John Cotton's Moses his Judicial and Abstract of the Laws of New England. Massachusetts Historical Society, Proceedings, 2nd series, vol. XVI.

Gay: Bryant's Popular History, vol. I, II.

Gay, Frederick L.: Rev. Francis Marbury. Massachusetts Historical Society, Collections, vol. 48.

Green, J. R.: Short History of The English People.

Greene, G. W.: History of Rhode Island.

Groome, Samuel: A Glass for the People of New England. Magazine of History. Extra number, 147. Tarrytown, N.Y.

Harleian Society Publications: Lincolnshire Pedigrees, vol. II.

Higginson, Francis: New England's Plantation. Young's Chronicles of Massachusetts.

Hosmer, James K.: Young Sir Harry Vane.

Howells, W. D.: Seven English Cities.

Hutchinson, Thomas: Anne Hutchinson in Massachusetts. Old South Leaflet.

Hutchinson, Thomas: History of Massachusetts, Appendix, vol. II.

Johnson, Edward: Wonder-Working Providence. W. F. Poole, *ed.*

Massachusetts Historical Society, Collections.

Massachusetts Historical Society, Proceedings.

Merburie's Tract, Prince Society Publications.

Murdock, Kenneth B.: Increase Mather.

New England Historical and Genealogical Register.

Old South Leaflets, nos. 21, 54, 164, 176, 178.

Palfrey, J. G.: New England, vol. I.

Parrington, V. L.: The Colonial Mind.

Portsmouth, R.I., Town Records.
Prince Society Publications.
Rhode Island Historical Society, Collections.
Roxbury, Mass., First Church Records.
Saintsbury, G. E. B.: Life of John Dryden.
Savage, James: A Genealogical Dictionary of the First Settlers of New England.
Shepard, Thomas: Autobiography. Nehemiah Adams, *ed.*
Shurtleff, N. B.: History of Old Building on Corner of School and Washington Streets.
Shurtleff, N. B.: List of the Printed Maps of Boston.
Shurtleff, N. B.: Records of the Governor and Company of the Massachusetts Bay.
Shurtleff, N. B.: A Topographical and Historical Description of Boston.
Thomas, J. M. Lloyd, *ed.*: The Autobiography of Richard Baxter.
Tyler, Moses Coit: A History of American Literature, 1607-1765.
Usher, Roland G.: The Pilgrims and their History.
Van Rensselaer, Mrs. Schuyler: History of the City of New York in the Seventeenth Century.
Walker, Williston: Ten New England Leaders.
Weld, Thomas: Introduction to Short History of the Rise . . . of the Antinomians. Prince Society Publications, XXI.
Welles, Lemuel A.: Site of Anne Hutchinson's Massacre. New York Genealogical and Biographical Records, vol. 60, no. 2.
Wendell, Barrett: Cotton Mather.
Wertenbaker, T. J.; The First Americans.
Wheelwright, John: Mercurius Americanus. Prince Society Publications.
Whitmore, W. H.: *See* Appleton.
Williams, Roger: Letters. Original MSS., John Carter Brown Library, Providence, R.I.
Winthrop, John: History of New England. James Savage, *ed.*
Winthrop, John: Short History of the Rise, Reign and Ruin of the Antinomians, etc. Introduction by Thomas Weld. C. F. Adams, *ed.*
Winthrop, R. C., Jr.: Life and Letters of John Winthrop.
Wood, William: New England's Prospect. Prince Society Publications.
Young, Alexander: Chronicles of Massachusetts.

INDEX

341